If this was heaven...

by Cynthia Jordan

Emerald Eagle Publishing

This book is lovingly dedicated to Marcus.
I call him, "My Happiness."

Table of Contents

Forward

It was the summer of 1997 when I first encountered, Cindy. We had both just moved to the Volunteer State of Tennessee, I from Geneva, Switzerland and Cindy from Texas. Cindy was brought up in California and I grew up in Luxembourg. Looking back all these years, I remember seeing a face just as lost as mine in a culture unfamiliar to both of us. United in an unshakable faith that things would get better, we started a friendship that continues to grow and last.

During the many hours I spent with Cindy I continued to be mesmerized by her optimism, her gratitude, and her love for life. Her brightness was such that I started calling her "Sunshine," reflecting the warmth and "joie de vivre" she provided for the ones around her. Being raised in a culture that looks at unshakable optimism with a rather critical eye, I was at first wondering whether she may simply be naïve or even superficial.

Despite my initial apprehension I had to admit that Sunshine had a secret and a gift that only a few of us are blessed with. It is the gift to see beauty in even the darkest moments; to remain faithful, even when everything seems lost. It is her steadfast belief in love, even when we may be surrounded by chaos and darkness.

In her most recent book "If This Was Heaven...," Sunshine shares some of the marvels she has been privileged to see in life with us, thereby inspiring and enlightening us to continue believing in beauty and love. Her short stories are captivating and refreshing, in reminding us that the world is a mesmerizing place after all and that beauty is in the eye of the beholder, therefore accessible to anyone at any time.
It has been quite a few years since Sunshine has moved back to Texas and despite missing her physical presence I am eternally grateful for her teachings. I frequently find myself using her metaphors, analogies, and humor in my work with human beings who have been forced to visit some of the darkest places imaginable to the human mind.

Sometimes, when I get caught up in the darkness, I guide myself back to light and love with one of Cindy's masterpieces; whether a song, a piano recital, or a story. I trust that this book will do the same for you and not only remind you of the beauty we encounter in this life, but provide you with hope in times of despair, love in times of fear and light in times of darkness.

Peace and Love,
Doctor Denise Reding-Jones, PhD
Licensed Psychologist, HSP, EMDR Certified
(Alias Moonbeam)

Intro

In the beginning there was God and only God. God is *Love.* Therefore in the beginning there was *Love* and only *Love. Love* wanted to experience itself so *Love* decided to create a being that would have the capability to feel love, make love and know love.

Love was invisible. Creation would have a physical form and the new being would be called *human. Love* would inhabit the human form and silently just "be". The *human being* would possess a spirit, a heart and intellect which would enable it to rationalize and experience all kinds of different emotions. Through these emotions *Love* would have the *human love experience.*

Love had some great ideas and was very excited. It wanted the human to be happy and enjoy the gift of life. *Love* designed and created a beautiful world, which the human would call "home". There would be deep blue oceans, grand mountains, scenic deserts and lush valleys. *Love* then created colorful flowers, and beautiful plants and trees to decorate the landscape.

After the "home" was finished *Love* created all kinds of wonderful animals to share this magnificent new world. The animals each had different lessons to teach the human and they would all live together in harmony. It was the most beautiful, magical place in the universe. *Love* called it Heaven. It was a perfect plan!

There was one more thing. *Love* needed to create an opposite to know itself better. Without contrast how could *Love* know itself? *Love's* great wisdom understood there must be darkness to know light. It needed a strong opposition based on fear so ego was created. Ego was made of fear and illusion.

Ego got its power by fooling the human into thinking that the value of the human was measured by the possession of things and a false sense of control. The ego also tricked the human into thinking there is a limited supply of everything including *Love.*

Finally the great day came and the plan was in action. It was time for *Love* to experience itself in human form. The human was created from *Love,* just as a flute is created from a tree. This would be remembered in magical moments of the human's life. *Love's* voice is silent, but the human would discover *Love* through the heart and soul where *Love* and the human are one.

Love could feel emotion and hear the human's thoughts. It could see, hear, taste and smell all of the beautiful things that had been created. It could feel the rain, the warmth of a fire and a loving kiss.

Love was experiencing life! Before *Love* had only existed but now it was *alive*! *Love* was *alive!*

Little by little, the human began to become aware of *Love.* The human began to realize there was a Great Intelligence that had created the world and stars and planets beyond. As the human became more aware it named *Love,* God. The humans have named the ego, Devil. It constantly challenges *Love* with trickery and false illusion.

There have been a few humans who have known *Love* and have become great teachers. One of them was a man named Jesus. Jesus said, "I am the light." His powerful message of *Love* has sustained for thousands of years.

Jesus taught us, "*Heaven is spread upon the earth and people do not see it.*" To see heaven all we have to do is look for *Love.* The soul knows this because our soul is one with God. The soul can see *"on earth as it is in heaven."* God is having the human experience through you. Are you showing God a good time?

The next time you pause at a sunset, be aware of the *silent observer* inside your heart watching through your eyes and loving you every moment of your life. You might want to say "Thank you God for painting this beautiful sunset to remind me you are with me."

However if you *listen* you might hear *Love's* silent voice say, "Thank you my child, for pausing to witness this beautiful sunset I created for you so that I could experience it through your eyes and feel the joy inside your heart and *our soul*. Together we are witnessing heaven on earth and it is just fine!"

A Jesus Day

Jesus is God spelling Himself out in language that men can understand. ~ S.D. Gordon

Ever had a day where you find something you really want on sale, hit all green lights, or think about someone you haven't talked to in a long time and they call? Sometimes you might even find something precious you thought was lost. My daughter Denise calls these, "Jesus days."

I believe you can have a "Jesus day" any day. Every day is full of miracles. The day I became aware of this, my life changed completely.

Here are seven things I do when I want to create a "Jesus day."

1. Count my blessings and say, "Thank you" for each one.
2. When challenged I ask myself, "What would love do now?"
3. Make a random, "I love you call," to someone I love.
4. Remind myself I am a spiritual being having the human experience.
5. Look at old photographs and reflect on good times.
6. Repeat "All is well" all day long.
7. Make choices as if it was my last day on earth.

God intended for our lives to be happy. I think when Jesus said, “The kingdom of heaven is within,” he was telling us that Love is the only thing that is real. Love can make any day a “Jesus day.” This is how we create heaven on earth and when we do, all is well.

Ahh Radio

Music is the organized flow of harmonic energy that resonates profoundly with the human spirit.
~ Cynthia Jordan

When I moved to San Angelo, Texas I didn't know a soul! Everything was brand new and we were learning about the community. One day my son, Jordan, came home excited. "Mom, I heard the best radio station! It plays music you like!" It was KCSA radio, 95.7 on the dial.

Jordan was right. KCSA radio had an open format and played a wonderful variety of music as well as old radio shows like "The Green Hornet" and "The Life of Riley". Because I am a composer and songwriter I figured I would go to the radio station and introduce myself. I love radio people and it seemed like a good place to start making friends. I met the Program Director, Rick and he invited me to lunch.

I had just moved to Texas from Nashville, where I had written and produced 11 instrumental CDs of relaxing piano music. After several months of doing research on the power of music, I had an idea.

Rick is a great guy and has decades of experience in radio. "I've always wanted to program a show that could sedate a city," I told him. "Playing two hours of beautiful instrumental music can help people sleep, relieve stress and even help students write better and retain more of what they read."

Rick looked at me and said, "Let's do it!"

I was kind of shocked. Nothing in the music business had ever come so easy.

"What do you want to call the show?" he asked.

"Let's call it *Ahh,*" I said with a grin.

Rick looked at me and asked, "Why Ahh?"

"What do you say at the end of a long day when you take off your shoes and get in a warm tub of bubbles or sink into your favorite chair?" I answered.

Rick smiled and said, "Ahhhhhhhh."

"Ahh" seems to be a universal sound that expresses things that are pleasing, happy or even divine.

What do we say when we see a toddler playing with a puppy or little booties…a new baby?

Awe!

What do we say when we have an enlightening moment?

Aha!

What do we say when we receive a sentimental gift?

Awe!

Usually the first word a baby says is, Mama. God, Yahweh, Jehovah all have the "ah" sound. Amor, Amen, Alleluia, Awesome are all "ah" words.

Ahh" is what we say when we feel peace.

I am very grateful to Rick for believing in my idea. In January of 2006 it began airing 9 to 11pm every evening. After a few months the show became so popular, Rick extended it to midnight.

Creating a radio show with soothing music for people to relax to has been fun. I especially love it when people recognize my voice at places like the grocery store and tell me they listen to the show. My listeners feel like friends I've never met.

One woman told me her husband goes to bed with me every night. I think it was a compliment.

Come visit me at aweradio.com. You might hear something like, "*Hi, this is your friend Cynthia. We're glad you're with us. We play beautiful music to awaken your spirit and soothe the soul.*"

I wonder if heaven has radio shows.

If there is one like "Ahh Radio" heaven will be just fine.

America the Beautiful

In 1893 Katharine Lee Bates was riding on a train to Pikes Peak in Colorado. As she looked upon the beautiful countryside surrounding her she was inspired to put her thoughts on paper. Within minutes her timeless words flowed from pen to paper.

O beautiful for spacious skies
For amber waves of grain
For purple mountain majesties
Above the fruited plain!
America! America!
God shed His grace on thee
And crown thy good with brotherhood
From sea to shining sea

Two years later Katherine's poem was published in The Congregationalist, to commemorate the Fourth of July. The poem was later applied to a melody written by Samuel Ward. The song is known as America the Beautiful and has been an expression of patriotism throughout the years.

When I hear these words I cannot help but think of those very brave European souls who first came to America. Most of them showed up after crossing the Atlantic Ocean on a boat with only a suitcase and a dream. Can you imagine what kind of courage this took? To me every one of them is a hero. They left everything they knew behind them knowing they would probably never see their homeland or families ever again. The dream of freedom and opportunity is the very foundation of our United States.

America speaks to my soul because the soul sings to the dance of freedom and completely resonates to the spirit of oneness. We are the United States of America. "Together we stand, divided we fall." Anyone who attempts to turn Americans against each other is not participating in the spirit of America.

If all Americans were only kind to each other, respectful and shared with loving hearts, I believe America would be heaven on earth.

I love America. It is in moments of witnessing her majestic beauty I like to say, "If this was heaven it would be just fine!"

Autumn Leaves

"Besides the autumn poets sing, A few prosaic days
A little this side of the snow and that side of the haze"
~Emily Dickinson

Native Americans have a beautiful legend that explains why leaves change into brilliant bright colors in the fall.

Many, many moons ago the great Creator made beautiful trees and flowers.

The flowers were made with the colors of the rainbow. Different variations of yellow, orange, red, pink, violet and blue decorated Earth Mothers fields with majestic splendor.

The trees were all green.

Some of the trees were very jealous of the flowers and they complained to Earth Mother.

"We want to be beautiful like the flowers!" they whined. "Green is boring."

Earth Mother loves all of her children and like any good mother she wants them to be happy.

"I will grant you your wish," Earth Mother said. ""However it is important to remember that everything we want, or think we want comes with a price to pay."

"We don't care," the trees exclaimed. "We just want to be beautiful."

Summer had ended and the coolness of the fall was in the air. The next morning the trees who wanted to be like the flowers awoke and found that their leaves had changed into bright beautiful colors.

They were so excited and became very vain. For many weeks the trees were satisfied. Some even argued that they were the prettiest.

"Look at me, I'm yellow!"

"I am so beautiful with my gorgeous orange leaves!"

"I am the most beautiful red tree in the forest!"

All the while the evergreens stayed true to themselves.

The days were becoming shorter and as the air became cooler the beautiful, bright colored leaves began to fall on the ground.

"Oh no my beautiful leaves are gone."

"I am so ugly, look at my bare branches!"

"How wish we were green again! Please, Earth Mother, change us back."

Earth Mother loves her children and wants them to be happy.

"Dear tree children, I will grant your wish. When spring is in the air you will be green again and will enjoy it throughout the summer. In the fall you will change into those beautiful colors you so desired. However, I told you there was a price to pay. In the winter months you will lose your leaves."

The evergreen trees never wanted to be anything else than what the great Creator had made them to be. They remain beautiful all the time.

I love the coolness of the fall and the brilliant colors of the leaves. There are many autumn days when I gaze at their beauty and say, “If this was heaven it would be just fine!”

Awaken the Spirit with Music

"Music gives a soul to the universe, wings to the mind, flight to the imagination and life to everything." ~ Plato

In the movie *Pretty Woman* there is a scene where Richard Gere has taken Julia Roberts on an elegant date to the Opera House in San Francisco. It is her first opera experience and she is completely engaged in the emotional impact of the drama. Although Julia's character doesn't understand the Italian lyrics, tears begin to roll down her cheeks as she hears the passion flow from the song being sung on stage.

As Richard Gere watches her tearful reaction you can see that he is impressed with her compassionate spirit. In a timeless moment the music takes them to that beautiful existence where souls are joined as one.

Music is the language of the spirit and spirit is everywhere. It speaks to us in the same way we feel when we see a beautiful sunset. Music comes in many forms. It is in the whisper of a breeze blowing through the leaves, the babbling of a brook flowing over ancient stones and the crackling of a fire on a dark, moonless night. Music is in the laughter of a child playing with a puppy, the gleeful song of the dolphin dancing in the waves and the sweet tune of small birds as they welcome the sun when beginning a new day.

Whenever music brings you joy, peace or a feeling of love you are experiencing, what I like to call, a "God thing." This is because God is everything that is good. We are all really spiritual beings having the human experience. Joy makes us celebrate that we are alive. Peace is our true nature and love is the very essence of God.

It is in that essence of spirit that we are one with our Creator. Whenever music causes you to feel joy, peace or love if you quiet your mind and listen, you might hear a voice whisper, "This is why we choose life". It is the voice of your highest self. Knowing this voice as your own is the magical awakening of the spirit.

Beautiful music can serve as a portal to your spiritual awareness and give you the feeling of heaven on earth. Knowing this can help you to connect with that part of you that is one with God.

God's voice is silent. It is the voice heard between the notes of the piano and the waves, softly breaking on the shore. It is the voice of your spirit. To hear it you must quiet the mind and just be. The next time you listen to beautiful music, sit still for a moment, breathe in deeply that precious gift of life and just be. You just might hear the silence say, "Thank you for the knowing that I am with you all-ways and life is good."

Babies

"Every child begins the world again."
~ Henry David Thoreau

I have always said there is no better way to see and understand God than through the eyes of a baby.

No matter what the circumstances are, a new baby is always a blessing. Pregnancy is a beautiful miracle.

My heart feels full and I get so excited when I hear God is creating a brand new little body to enable a soul to have the human experience.

When I get the news that someone is pregnant I always say, "That's awesome! Babies are always a blessing!" I think Jesus would say the same thing. Jesus so loved little children and babies.

Life is about new babies and the people we love.

Next time you see a baby, look for your reflection in their eyes. It's magical when you do it with a loving heart. When I do it I can see the miracle of life and I celebrate a loving God.

I love to sing little babies to sleep. I love the way they smell and the softness of their little heads. I love the way babies snuggle and the sounds they make when they breathe.

Yes dear friends, whenever I hold a little baby I think, "If this was heaven it would be just fine!"

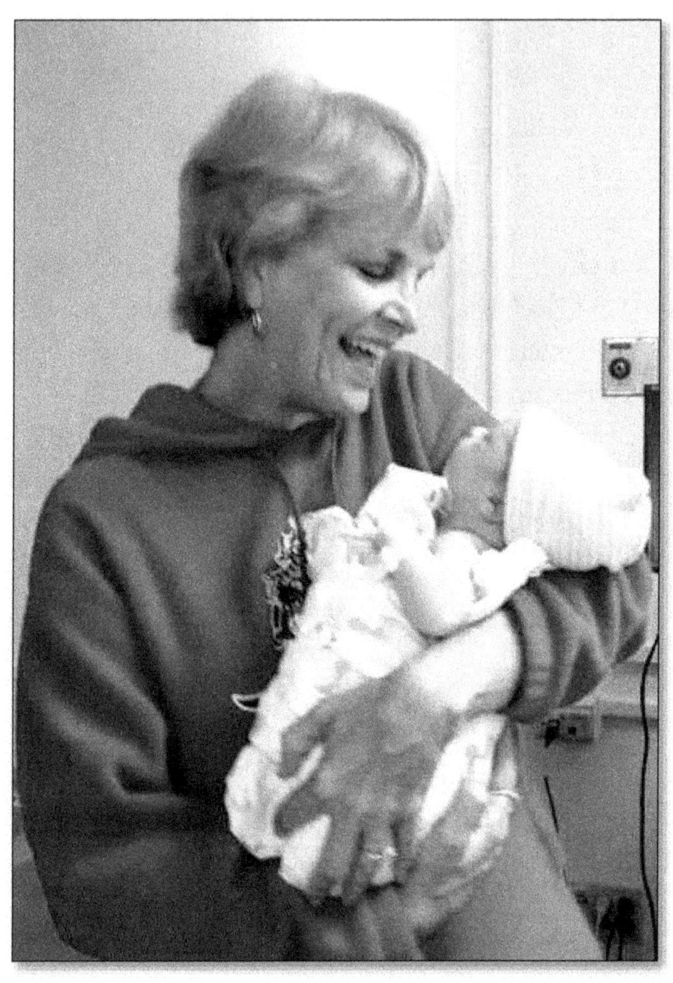

"Welcome to the world little Sarah.
I am your Nana."

Born Again

"Most assuredly, I say to you, unless one is born again, he cannot see the kingdom of God." ~ John 3:3

When I was a little girl Santa Claus brought me an etch-a-sketch. It was a rectangular toy that had a red frame surrounding a gray screen. There were two dials on it, one made vertical lines and the other made horizontal lines. If you didn't like the picture you were making you could simply shake the etch-a-sketch and the screen would completely clear.

Sometimes things happen in our lives that we wish we could erase. Some of those things are personal regrets and some are things others have done. I have found forgiveness is the most powerful way to clean your screen.

Jesus said it perfectly when he taught us to pray. "Forgive us our trespasses as we forgive those who trespass against us." When we forgive others we let go of resentment and anger. When we forgive ourselves we let go of guilt. Both are toxic to the soul.

Sometimes people have a hard time forgiving. This is completely understandable. Many people think when we forgive we are somehow saying the violation was justified. The ego is completely opposed to forgiveness. It takes a very strong soul to be able to forgive. I had the privilege to meet such a soul.

Her name is Immaculée Ilibagiza. She was born in Rwanda and in 1994 survived the Rwanda genocide when for 91 days she and seven other women huddled silently together in a small bathroom of a local pastor's house. During this horrific ordeal, most of Immaculée's family was slaughtered.

While scrunched up in that bathroom Immaculée learned English by reading the bible. She was deeply touched by the words Jesus said from the cross. "Father, forgive them! They know not what they do."

After she was liberated she had the opportunity to visit a man in jail who was partly responsible for killing her family. Instead of confronting the man with anger and hate she told him he was forgiven. The prison guard actually was upset that Immaculée didn't get angry at him. Her story of forgiveness written in her book, *Left to Tell* has made a major impact in changing lives all over the world.

When I met Immaculée I had created a surprise presentation for her with photos of Immaculée and the people and beauty of Rwanda. The song "You Raise Me Up" played behind the slideshow. She was deeply moved and we both cried together as Bishop Pfeifer held her hand. I am honored to say she went on to show that same DVD at the end of her presentations. She also included my version of the Ave Maria on her rosary CD where she says the rosary partly in her native tongue and it is beautiful. I know Immaculée has had a huge impact on my life with her story of her miraculous transition into forgiveness and beautiful relationship with God.

Could you do what Immaculée did? Can you imagine the strength that took? So many can't forgive even for reasons much less severe.

When we carry someone else's toxic words or actions around with us it's like smearing their garbage and toxic waste all over ourselves. Resentment causes stress and pain and can cause us to be offensive to people we encounter and love.

Victims never have the right to violate. Prisons are full of people like that. Some people don't want to forgive because they want something or someone to blame.

That's crazy! When we forgive we are washed clean. We are born again. It can be very liberating! Forgiveness cleans the soul and creates a perfect, beautiful space for love to come into your heart.

If you have a problem with forgiveness try saying something like, "This is for-giving it back to you. I am reclaiming my power with the love and beautiful light of God. Those were your words or actions. I don't want to own them anymore!"

You can even do a ceremony. Write down what you are forgiving on a piece of paper and burn it. I have even been known to flush it down the toilet. Something about that swishing round and round and then disappearing forever into the sewer where it belongs is so satisfying!

Jesus forgave his persecutors. God is always ready to forgive. Therefore when we forgive we are doing what I like to call "A God thing."

The ego is weak. Love is strong. If you need forgiveness from someone who is unwilling to forgive, just forgive them. Just remember the ego hates forgiveness. Love can fix anything. Just like that etch-a-sketch you have the power to wipe the slate clean. If you have been violated maybe it's time to finally get rid of it.

If Immaculée can do it, you can too. I promise it will make you feel born again and set you free! Then your spirit will dance in the light of love with peace and joy on earth as it is in heaven.

Then as you feel the peace fill your heart give thanks and say, "If this was heaven it would be just fine!"

Choctaw

"If you have faith as a grain of mustard seed, you will say to your mountain, "Move!" and it will move...and nothing will be impossible for you!" ~ Matthew 17:20

One of the greatest teachers in my life is a man I call Choctaw. When Choctaw was about fifteen years old, he was hitchhiking home when a very nice sedan pulled over and picked him up. A girl from his high school was sitting in the back seat of the car. She had recognized him and her father stopped to give him a ride. Choctaw slid into the backseat next to her. The family was one of the more affluent families in the county and she was one of the prettiest girls in the school.

Choctaw was feeling pretty cool about riding in a big car with such a fine family and the conversation was going pretty well. All of a sudden the pretty little teenage girl started laughing. "He's not wearing any shoes, Daddy!"

Choctaw laughed right along with them. It was cold outside, and she thought it was funny he didn't have any shoes on. The reason he had no shoes was far from her reality and she thought it was strange in a quirky kind of way.

Choctaw made up some kind of clever excuse about not having his shoes and everyone in the car had a great laugh together. They let him off at a place close to his home. He smiled, thanked them for the ride and waved goodbye.

As the car drove away, tears of frustration and shame rolled down his face.

Choctaw cried all the way home. The reason he wasn't wearing any shoes was because his family could not afford them. He made the decision right then and there that he would one day escape his prison of poverty. He became motivated and determined to change his reality.

I am not sure if Choctaw ever finished high school but I do know that he just sold one of his companies for over 60 million dollars. Today, Choctaw pretty much owns most of that small town in Arkansas where he had his most humble beginnings.

I asked Choctaw his philosophy on success. He held up three fingers and said, "It takes three steps Cindy. First you dream, then the struggle and finally, the reward." Choctaw shuddered and shook his head when he said the word struggle. Choctaw's philosophy is simple. This doesn't mean it's easy. When that reward finally shows up Choctaw will tell you, "The best part is the knowing that all things are possible with God." When you partner with God you experience "earth as it is in heaven" and it's just fine.

The Circle Game

I always loved this song by Joni Mitchell. I added a few verses. The seasons of our life are learning stages to discover we are really divine spiritual beings. When we finally know this we live our lives on earth as it is in heaven it is just fine!

Yesterday a child came out to wander
Chasing butterflies and running free
Living in the moment feeling happy
Laughter singing joyful in the breeze

(chorus)
And the wheels they go round and round
And the painted ponies go up and down
We're captive on the carousel of time
We can't return we can only look
behind from where we came
And go round and round and round
In the circle game

Then the child moved through many seasons
Skated over many frozen streams
Words like "when you're older" must appease him
And promises of someday make his dreams
(chorus)

The years spin by and now the child is 30
Though dreams have lost their grandeur coming true
Now there are new dreams, dreams of plenty
Again we see another year is through
(chorus)

It seems not long the child now is 50
Looking back on life the journey made
Seeing now with different eyes of wonder
Dancing now in the light of the circle game
(chorus)

Years have passed the child now is 80
Quiet in a dream of golden years
Lines upon a face that tell a story
Of happiness, love and silent tears
(chorus)

Now the child has lived beyond loved ones
It's time to pass from here into the light
Through the veil again to be with loved ones
And dancing in a brand new body bright
(chorus)

Compliments and Appreciation

"For each new morning with its light,
For rest and shelter of the night,
For health and food, for love and friends,
For everything Thy goodness sends."
~Ralph Waldo Emerson

Have you ever given someone a gift and felt unappreciated?

Did they somehow make you think your gift wasn't good enough?

How did this make you feel?

Did it make you want to give them anything else?

Negative people are no fun to be around.

What about that person who loves everything you give them?

Does their appreciation make you want to give them more?

Of course!

Gratitude is the most powerful vibration in the entire universe. It is like a magnet. The more you appreciate your blessings the more blessings come your way.

"I appreciate you," is a beautiful, effortless gift and so easy to say. I like to say it to God all the time.

To me it's just like saying, "I love you" and in many cases can even be more meaningful.

I don't understand why so many times people only express dissatisfaction and forget to compliment or even say "thank you." When you give unconditionally like God does, it really doesn't matter. It reminds me of the story of the ten lepers who come to Jesus to be healed. After Jesus healed them only one said, "thank you." Unbelievable!

I think it's important to let the people you love know how much you appreciate them. I have worked with children for many years. I have learned that complimenting them when they are doing something right makes them want to do more good.

I think calling children negative names is unproductive. Whenever my son Jordan would need to be corrected I would always say, "Jordan, you're such a good boy. Why did you do that?"

Adults are no different. Good leaders know that compliments and appreciation will always evoke better productivity. You can always find something good to say about someone.

A compliment is always a gift. Saying, "Thank you," is also a gift. It makes the one who gives the compliment feel good. Some people don't understand this. One day when I was in high school I told a girl I liked her new hair style. Her response was, "I had to put it up because it's so dirty." The rest of the day every time I saw her I only saw dirty hair.

My dad tells the story of a man who walked into his friend's house and said, "What a beautiful home!"

"Yeah, all except for that crack in my ceiling," his friend responded.

From then on every time the man visited his friend he would look up and say, “I see you still haven’t fixed that crack in your ceiling.”

I remember a story in Chicken Soup for the Soul. A teacher passed out a paper that had the names of every student in the class on it. The assignment was to write something you admired about that person next to their name. She then gave each student their personal list of compliments. Years later at a classmate’s funeral, several of the attendees had their lists with them. The young man, who had passed away, serving his country in Viet Nam, also had his list with him when he died.

Just think if everyone in the world could focus on the good in people with love and appreciation. This is how Jesus sees everyone.

If everyone could become a *professional complimentor* and appreciate their blessings I believe we could create a world full of harmony and love.

Whenever I receive a compliment I always say, “Thank you. You just made my day!” Then as I am basking in my moment of happiness I think, “That made my heart feel good. If this was heaven it would be just fine!”

C.V. and Ellis Mae

"Yea, though I walk through the valley of the shadow of death, I will fear no evil: for thou art with me; Thy rod and thy staff they comfort me."
--Psalms 23:4

It was Wednesday, November 3rd, 1971 the morning Cecil Van Payne called his daughter's house and said he wanted to go to the hospital. Cecil known to his beloved family as Pa Payne was my husband Dennis's maternal grandfather. Somehow he knew it was the last day of his life.

"What's wrong, Pa?" his daughter Wanda asked.

"I need to go to the hospital," Pa answered.

Pa seemed normal as ever. He had taken off his rings and watch and placed them on a sideboard in his bedroom along with his billfold. He signed four checks for his loving wife, Ellis Mae, who had never signed a check before in the 50 years of their married life. He was ready to go.

"But, there's nothing wrong with you!" everyone kept saying. There was no problem with his heart or breathing. Looking back maybe it was just wishful thinking. "If my dad says he has to go to the hospital than he has to go to the hospital!" Wanda insisted. She was his only child, known to us as Grannie, and she always got her way.

They had called the family physician, Doctor Follis. He had brought all five of Wanda's children, three boys and two girls, into the world. After some conversation the ambulance took Pa Payne and the family brought Mom Payne to the hospital with them.

At the hospital, Doctor Follis examined him and all his vital signs seemed normal. "There's nothing wrong with you Mr. Payne. You can go home."

Again Wanda intervened. "If my dad says he needs to be in the hospital than he will stay."

Doctor Follis was a little bewildered. "OK, I guess it won't hurt anything."

That afternoon at 2:30 pm Pa Payne closed his eyes and peacefully passed.

The family was sad but somehow they managed to make it through Christmas. Mom Payne loved Christmas and laughed her beautiful laugh through the holidays. She used to throw her head back with a big "Wah Ha Ha Ha!" Her laughter was like happy music. She made the best of things for her family's sake, but she was secretly missing the love of her life.

Finally, on March 3rd 1972, just four months to the day after her husband's passing, Ellis Mae Payne called the house to tell her family, "goodbye."

"I'm going home to see Pa," she said. "I miss him."

The next day Ellis Mae Payne joined her beloved C.V.

I wonder what she saw when they were reunited. I know the love was there. Since then their daughter Wanda, Dennis's mother has joined them in the celestial realm.

How did Pa Payne and Mom Payne know it was their time? I guess some people just do. To me the most beautiful part of their story is that there was no fear at all. There was only love. I know Pa Payne's cane was gone and he was standing straight and tall as he welcomed his beautiful Ellis Mae to her new home in heaven. Maybe she looked like the day they were married when she was only eighteen years old.

I think the most beautiful thing about growing old together is the fact that we still see those we love in their youth especially in their eyes and their beautiful smile. When the spirit glows in the light of love there is no such thing as age.

Love is heaven on earth and this makes everything here just fine.

CV and Ellis Mae with their daughter Wanda

Darkness and Light

"I have never in my life learned anything from any man who agreed with me."
~Dudley Field Malone

To really know anything well, you must first experience its opposite. God created light from the darkness.

I was speaking at a women's luncheon in Nashville, Tennessee. We were in a beautiful room with great big windows. I asked the ladies to look outside and tell me how many stars were out. They collectively said, "None."

I smiled and said, "There are millions of stars out. We just can't see them because the sun is shining so bright."

When the night sky is the darkest and there is no moon at all, it seems like the stars twinkle and shine the brightest. It has been in my darkest moments that I have searched to find the loving light of God. Although it may take some time to understand, *why*, God never lets me down.

I have learned, the greater the challenge, the greater the opportunity to know and completely trust God.

When my daughter, Denise, was 5 years old a young horse was getting up from its side and she was accidentally kicked in the head. Denise was thrown across the barn and her little body slid down the wall unconscious. When she finally came to, she was completely blind.

On the way to the hospital I remember feeling so small. I started talking to God.

"I'm not going to insult your intelligence! You know what I want. There are three options. Denise will either die, be permanently blind or everything will turn out great. If you decide it will be either one of the first two, I just ask that you give me the strength I will need to deal with it."

It was the day I learned how to pray.

That evening Denise was able to see light again. By morning her sight had completely returned.

"Hi Mommy," was music to my ears.

When I go to heaven I want to hear, "Hi Mommy," just like I did that morning I knew my baby was going to be OK. If heaven plays that kind of music, heaven will be just fine.

Disneyland

"There is just one moon and a golden sun
And a smile means friendship to everyone
Though the mountains are high
And the oceans are wide
It's a small world after all"
~ Disneyland ride

I remember I was at a spiritual retreat in Michigan one time. We were in a lovely home and there was a very simple two dimensional map of the earth hanging on the wall. The land was green and the oceans and seas were blue.

The woman facilitator was pointing to different continents and there was an ongoing conversation about all of the chaos, wars and hunger happening in different areas of the world. When it was my turn to speak she pointed at the picture and asked me "what do you see?"

"I see Disneyland," I told her. "I love the fact there are no lines or borders. I see a beautiful playground filled with mountains, rivers, oceans and waterfalls. I see green grass, beautiful flowers, majestic trees, plenty of food, and furry animals." I remember she just looked at me. I had offered a different perception and the energy of the whole room shifted.

Walt Disney's mission statement was simply, "to make people happy." I think God created earth like Walt

Disney created Disneyland, a beautiful place for people to be happy.

Nature is in perfect order. Man is the cause of chaos. If people would simply, "Love thy neighbor," like Jesus told us to, it would be an absolutely perfect place to live!"

Dear friends, may I suggest today and every day that you turn on your love light for everyone. God gives an unlimited supply of love to every single human being on this earth equally and unconditionally, including you.

"Love your enemies." They're not really enemies. They are just confused people who do not know or really understand God's great love. People who do are generous, forgiving and kind to everyone, are just like Jesus.

Live with your love light quietly shining on everyone you know or meet. Then when you look out the window or walk out into God's beautiful earth we call home, you might say, "If this was heaven it would be just fine!"

Dream Stealers

"Don't make the good opinion of others
become your reality."
~ Les Brown

"I gotta see it, to believe it!"
"That's impossible!"
"No way."
"You can't do that!"
"That will never work."
"I heard..."
"Blah blah blah, na nan na etc."

Sadly enough most people will buy into the negative opinion of others with absolutely no investigation of their own. This makes new ideas vulnerable to opposition purely on hearsay alone. Phrases like "They say," or "I read," somehow validate their negative input and people actually buy into it.

I have learned that what people say is their reality. If someone says you can't do something there is usually some kind of fear (ego) attached. They don't want to lose you... maybe you'll show them up or most often they see themselves able to accomplish what you are attempting to do.

It is important for you to discover your own truth? The question is, "When does it become important enough to investigate?"

It takes tremendous courage to be willing to fail. However there has never been a great accomplishment without some challenges along the way. Breaking a paradigm is not easy.

History shows us what visionaries and explorers like Columbus went through to prove the earth was a sphere when Western Europe believed the earth was flat. Galileo was put into prison when he affirmed Copernicus's Theory that it is the sun, not the earth that is the center of our solar system. It takes a lot of courage to promote change.

The ego hates to be wrong and therefore resists the chance that it may be fooled. Change is uncomfortable for many, especially the older we get. Old reeds are brittle and stand stiff, whereas young reeds are flexible and bend in the wind. For this very reason Jesus advised us to see the world through the eyes of young children. A child sees every day as a brand new adventure.

There are no guarantees, only a fascination with life and all it has to offer. It is an incredible journey. Don't miss the chance to experience all that you can. Sometimes It may seem like you are walking in the darkness, but you never are. God is all ways with you and you are never alone. Heaven is where God is and it is wonderful!

Eagles and Chickens

"The day is done, and the darkness,
Falls from the wings of Night,
As a feather is wafted downward,
From an eagle in his flight"
~Henry Wadsworth Longfellow

One day a man was walking down the road and saw an eagle's egg lying on the ground. He took the egg to a nearby farm.

Several months later he went back to the farm and saw the eagle on the ground squawking and pecking with the other chickens.

"Why is the eagle pecking on the ground," he asked the farmer.

"He thinks he's a chicken," the farmer said.

The man took the eagle to the fence post and said, "Fly with the wind beneath your wings. You are an eagle!"

The eagle looked around, spread his wings and hopped down and began scratching the ground again with the other chickens.

Then the man took the eagle to the top of the barn. "Fly with the wind beneath your wings. You are an eagle, the king of all birds!"

The eagle stood tall, looked around, spread his wings then slid down the roof and resumed pecking with the chickens.

Then the man put the eagle on his arm and walked high up into the canyon. When they reached the top the view was breath taking. All that could be heard was the wind gently singing through the crisp cool air.

"Fly with the wind beneath your wings. You are an eagle! You are king of the sky!"

The eagle looked at the beautiful valley below and then looked into the sky. The man lifted his arm and with that, the eagle spread his wings and flew over the vast canyon with grace and majesty!

My friend Tamara called me the other day and told me she was kicked out of a girl club. She was broken hearted. One girl had positioned Tammy as a common enemy and the group turned against her. My friend had been *mean-girled* out of the club.

I told her, "You don't belong with them, Tam. You are an eagle! You make a real lousy chicken!" Then I told her this story.

She laughed.

In the book of John, Jesus says, *"I tell you the truth, anyone who has faith in me will do what I have been doing. He will do even greater things than these, because I am going to the Father."*

Sometimes I fly like an eagle in my dreams. The feeling is exhilarating! I believe I will be able to fly like an eagle in heaven, and when I do, heaven will be just fine!

Expansion

"They are the sons and daughters of life's longing for itself.
They come through you but not from you,
and though they are with you yet they belong not to you.
You may give them your love but not your thoughts,
For they have their own thoughts."
~ Kahlil Gibran

My children have been my best teachers. They are my greatest inspiration and I am in awe of all of them. Julie is a self-motivator. She lived in Europe for ten years, is fluent in French and Italian and has her CPA. She has worked hard for her accomplishments and has motivated me to expand myself. I love it when she says, "Let's focus on the solution Mom, not the problem."

Denise is my poster child in overcoming adversity. She is a hero to me and she motivates me to expand myself to be the best that I can be especially when it comes to integrity. She is a survivor and meets her challenges with insurmountable courage and grace. I love the way she calls me, "Mommy."

My son, Jordan, has an inquisitive mind and all his life he has presented me with amazing theories and questions. When he was five-years-old his dog died and we had a small funeral ceremony on the ranch. Later that day while Dennis was working on his car Jordan approached him with solemn contemplation.

"Does everybody have to die?" he asked his Dad.

"Yes, son… everybody has to die," Dennis answered like daddies do.

Jordan was quiet for a few minutes. My husband could see those wheels in his head spinning away.

Finally after a few minutes Jordan said, "I guess you know the last one to die isn't going to get buried." He had thought it all the way through.

By the time Jordan was ten it was very clear that his thoughts were of an expansive nature and out of the box. I love that about him. One day as we were driving down the road I said, "Jordan, I want you to know that I am the kind of mom that you can tell me anything and I won't think you're weird."

After a few minutes he looked at me and said, "Good Mom! You know there's no such thing as time!"

"Really!" I said. "I think Einstein said the same thing."

Just yesterday Jordan wrote me an email on the subject of expansion with some thoughts that really impressed me. It opened up a new dimension of understanding and thought that I am grateful for. I'd like to share a portion of that email with you now.

"In ultimate reality, Love is all that exists. Every experience we can possibly have in the physical universe is wonderful – because it allows the nonphysical part of ourselves its ultimate goal – EXPANSION!

Even experiences that we may perceive to be terrible from the limited perception of our conscious minds are at their base absolutely magnificent because they allow us the expansion which we constantly seek. Your children are not your children.

In times of our greatest trials can come our greatest triumphs.

In times of our greatest joy can come our greatest gains.

From beautiful heights we can have the expansive experience of knowing who we truly are.

From the depths of despair we can still achieve fantastic expansion! This is the great dichotomy of life.

All experiences allow expansion. The greater the intensity of the experience, the greater the expansion!

It doesn't matter how we perceive a situation, it is always allowing expansion. As we expand, the whole of God expands. It is in this way that all things can be beautiful and magnificent.

It is in this place that we may find ultimate freedom."
~ Jordan Buckingham

I have encouraged Jordan to write *his* book. He has a burning desire to empower people and I am convinced he will do just that. He has already helped to empower me.

If you have children I encourage you to listen to them. The world belongs to them and the generations to come. I feel there is a new breed of children born every day with the purpose of creating heaven on earth. We need to do what it takes to encourage, mentor and make this happen. Jesus told us we can do it. He taught us that all things are possible with God.

Earth is a beautiful place. It belongs to our children and grandchildren. Love and kindness is a great place to start to create "on earth as it is in heaven."

Every day of your life look for heaven on earth in those beautiful moments of love and appreciation for God's creation. When you do let God know you are thankful and say, "If this was heaven I believe it will be just fine!" It will make God smile.

Jordan with his sister Denise the day she finished boot camp.

Fish and Turtles

"The only source of knowledge is experience."
~ Albert Einstein

I have learned the only way to really know something, is to experience it. But to really, really, really know something you need to experience the opposite. Fish don't know they are wet. This is because they have never experienced dry. Turtles on the other hand know the difference.

If you could live your life over is there anything you would change or not do again? Most of us would probably say, yes. I know there are things I have done that I would certainly *never* do again. In each experience God was there.

I really like the word atonement (at-one-ment). The more I am aware of my oneness with God, the more I make my choices from the *Love* place. I have forgiven myself for all those times that I made bad choices. Although my bad choices are painful memories I am grateful for every one of them because they have taught me what I am not.

I have learned there is a loving, silent observer within each of us that experiences *everything we do,* including the dark moments. This silent observer is our oneness with God. It feels our emotions, it witnesses through our eyes, and it hears every thought and memory in our minds.

I have also learned to take responsibility for my feelings. Now when I get upset or have a negative thought about someone else I ask myself, "What needs to be healed or forgiven in me that makes me so passionately upset with this person who is just being who they are?"

God is Love and always feels good. Fear is ego and always feels bad to someone. So my dear friends, next time someone or something makes you feel bad, find the Love. Self -reflection will clear the way and forgiveness will empower you.

When we walk on the path of Love it's just like heaven and it feels just fine.

Frozen Faces

Peace begins with a smile..."
~ Mother Teresa

I have played music in many different venues. One of my favorite places to play is Assisted Living homes. People in their golden years have amazing stories. They are survivors of history and I think of them as precious treasures. I especially love to watch their faces light up when I sing a song that revives an old memory. Sometimes they will tell me how it reminds them of a loved one who has passed.

People tell me all the time that they like my smile. There are three reasons I smile all the time:

1. I like people who smile a lot
2. I read one time a smile is an instant facelift
3. I want my frozen face to be pleasant

What's a frozen face? It's the face you have when you think no one is looking.

The older we get the more our frozen face freezes. This is the most obvious with people over seventy. When I go to the assisted living homes I can pretty much tell what kind of a life that person has had by their frozen face.

Personally I want people to think of me as a happy person so I tend to smile a lot. If I'm upset about something I try to smile even bigger.

What does your frozen face look like?

I'll bet there are lots of smiles in heaven.

God smiles when you smile.

A smile is a sign of contentment and joy. A smile can be a gift of love.

Since God is love and heaven is where God is when we smile we create heaven on earth and it's just fine!

German Chocolate Cake

"All that I am or hope to be, I owe to my angel mother."
Abraham Lincoln

All events of every day are a blessing. This is because life itself is a gift. Pain, fear and even things that seem like a major catastrophe all have some kind of divine purpose. Most of the time we do not understand the lesson until some time has passed. But sometimes you can see the blessing right away. Yes, everything really does happen for a reason.

I was in the Dallas Airport with about 35 other people waiting to board our flight on a turbo jet to San Angelo. Because of the bad weather, our flight was postponed several times. Finally, we all boarded several hours later than our scheduled flight. Those of us who reside in San Angelo were almost glad for the storm as we needed the rain so desperately after a three digit dry summer. About 50 miles from home the pilot came on the radio and announced that we had been diverted to Abilene, Texas where we would be spending the night.

We were safe and it was raining in San Angelo. Hooray! In my mind all was well. I really love Texans and for the most part we were all visiting and even having fun. There was a baby girl named Lily who was on her way to meet her maternal grandmother for the first time. She was adorable and a light to the whole ordeal. I was singing songs of course and talking to people. Nobody seemed grumpy and it turned out to be a memorable and even uplifting experience.

It was amazing how we all bonded. We were all in it together and I couldn't help but wonder how this alteration in our plans affected every individual there and those families, friends and businesses waiting at our destination. Each one of us can finish the sentence, "If our flight had not been delayed then I wouldn't have…"

For me this was, "If our flight had not been delayed then I wouldn't have my two new friends, Sherri and Susan."

When God orchestrates a synchronized series of events that hold a message of love, it is a beautiful gift from heaven. When we look for and recognize the blessings in every experience, we are living our life in a state of appreciation and trust of God's will. This is the highest vibration in the entire universe.

The next morning after spending the night in Abilene, we were finally homeward bound. Sherri was sitting on my left at the window and Susan was on my right sitting in the aisle seat. Susan was telling us that she was opening a cake and baking business.

"What is your favorite cake you like to bake?" I asked.

"My carrot cake!" Susan answered with pride. She went on to describe how she makes it.

"Do you make German Chocolate cakes?" Sherri asked.

"I sure do," Susan said.

"Oh. That's awesome. I love German Chocolate cake. Every year on my birthday it was a tradition for my mother to bake me a German Chocolate cake. My mother is gone now and I really miss her baking my special cake on my birthday. Her frosting was just like candy."

As she was speaking Susan was nodding her head. "My frosting tastes like candy as well," she said with a smile. "I know how you feel. I lost my mother last October and I really miss her."

"My birthday is tomorrow," Sherri said with a sigh. "I will miss Mom's cake."

I bet you can guess what came flying out of Susan's mouth next.

"I'm going to make you a birthday cake!" Susan said clapping her hands with a great big smile.

I could hear the wheels of the plane release as the plane approached a very smooth and long awaited landing. We were home!

"Oh no!" Sherri said with embarrassment. "I didn't mean for you to bake me a cake. No, no no!" She kept repeating it.

For every "no" Sherri said, Susan was that more determined to make that cake.

"Sherry," I finally said. "You need to give Susan the opportunity to give love to you! Don't you see what has happened here? Your Mother is making sure you get your German Chocolate cake!"

The next day Susan gave Sherri her birthday cake and it was delicious! Somehow the three of us have kept in touch and in reflection all of us agree it was a magical moment.

Susan says, “What a blessing it was to meet you both and bake Sherri her cake.”

Sherri says, “It was a beautiful random act of kindness.”

I think Sherri’s mother asked God to make it happen. Sherri’s Mom said, “God, I want my little girl to have a German Chocolate cake for her birthday and I’m not there to give it to her.” Then God said, “I know a woman who can make it who is on the same flight as Sherri. Tell you what I’ll do…”

“If they make German Chocolate birthday cakes in heaven, heaven will be just fine!”

I’ll bet her mother will have one waiting for her when she finally arrives.

Girl Scouts 1942

"On my honor, I will try
To serve God and my country,
To help people at all times,
And to live by the Girl Scout Law."
~ The Girl Scout Promise

I love the way God creates events that make dreams come true. I believe the miracles that seem like small coincidences have the greatest lessons. These are the ones that are so simple they can easily be overlooked and recognized as the answer to a prayer. Children are aware of these types of miracles and we can learn much from their pureness of heart.

It was the fall of 1942 and little Margie Solis (my Mom) was ten-years-old. Only a few months before the United States had gotten involved in World War II and it was an emotional time for Americans. In the spirit of patriotism little Margie had a secret desire to be a girl scout.

She knew that money was tight. People were spending their money on only bare essentials and a Girl Scout uniform was certainly not on the list of important things to ask for. Still Little Margie never gave up her dream.

Margie lived in Redondo Beach, California. On weekends her parents allowed her to take the Sunset Stage bus to go to the theatre in Hermosa, a few miles away. The cost was about ten cents to get into to the show and Margie loved to go.

One Saturday afternoon after getting off the bus Margie noticed a small black cloth coin purse on the sidewalk. She opened it and looked inside. To her delight Margie found $12.00! It was like finding a treasure. It was enough money to buy a Girl Scout uniform!

What do you think she did with the money? What any honorable girl scout would do of course! She turned it into the police station. In fact it just happened to be on the same block where she found the money.

A very kind officer told little Margie that if no one claimed the money in the next two weeks she could have it. Sure enough, two weeks passed and the phone rang with the good news. No one had claimed the money and little Margie's dream of becoming a girl scout came true.

Margie's mother took her to JC Penney's that week to buy her uniform, a belt, socks, a tie, a beret, a sash and an official girl scout handbook. She got the works and the bill was just about exactly $12.00.

Margie went on to be the song leader of the Busy Bee Patrol and spent several years in the girl scouts. Because Margie is my mother, I naturally became a brownie in the second grade. It was one of the best experiences of my youth.

Mom is extremely patriotic. Fourth of July is her favorite holiday. She has over a hundred flags she likes to put out every year for decorations. One day I asked her, "Why did you want to be a girl scout?"

"I just did," she answered as if I had asked her, "Why do you like breathing?"

In those days it was a different time of patriotism and appreciation for this wonderful country we live in I like to think of as, The United States, emphasis on United.

I love this story about my Mom. When she turned in that money, Little Margie was already living by the Girl Scout *Law:*

I will do my best to be
Honest and Fair,
Friendly and Helpful,
Considerate and Caring,
Courageous and Strong, and
Responsible for what I say and do,
And to respect myself and others,
respect authority, use resources wisely,
make the world a better place, and
be a sister to every Girl Scout

Some of my favorite memories of my childhood are from the days when I was a girl scout. I even learned to play the guitar so I could play for my friends as we sat around the campfire. I taught my Girl Scout friends the songs my mother taught me. After all she was the song leader of the *Busy Bee Patrol.*

I'll bet there are girl scouts in heaven singing around campfires. It is surely a time I'd like to experience again. One day I will surely join them and when I do it will be just fine.

Go With the Flow

"Don't worry 'bout a thing
'Cause every little thing's gonna be alright."
~Bob Marley

Wouldn't it be awesome if we could choose any day we want to relive in heaven? One of the thousands of days I would love to visit again was a day in the fall of 1975. I was visiting my friend, Lerin, in New Mexico. We had packed a picnic to go on a canoe ride in the canyon. This was a brand new experience for me.

New Mexico is truly "the land of enchantment." As we floated down the river I remember thinking I had never experienced peace like this before. Lerin's friend, Ivor, pointed out an eagle flying into her nest positioned high above in the canyon walls. Even thinking about it now fills me up. I had never seen an eagle before.

I was in awe of the beauty surrounding me and I felt a deep appreciation for nature's blessings. As Ivor paddled the canoe, I thought of the thousands of years Native Americans drifted peacefully on this river.

The day inspired the lyrics to my song, "Go with the Flow." I actually wrote the chorus in a dream. To this day it is still one of Lerin's favorite songs

The memory of that magical day remains fondly in my heart. If heaven allows us to relive our days on earth I will certainly choose that day as one to experience again.

When I do I will surely say, "This is heaven and this is just fine!"

Go With the Flow

words and music by Cynthia Jordan

Too many things are running through your mind
And you're worried about things you cannot change
Sometimes you just want to run away and hide
But when you return they will all be the same
Just realize what is just is
It's a perfect world because the plan is His
Let's go where the wind blows through the canyon
And the eagle flies so high above the sky
I will show you a peaceful place on the river
And we'll drift away where you can ease your mind
Some people say that I am chasing rainbows
And they try to steal my dreams away
But I know there's magic when you believe in miracles
And you can see them each and every day

God Doesn't Make No Junk

"Any fool can count the seeds in an apple.
Only God can count all the apples in one seed."
~Robert H. Schuler

I once saw a cartoon of a toddler dragging his blanket. The caption read, "I must be perfect, 'cause God doesn't make no junk!"

I never forgot that.

I have never agreed with the phrase, "Nobody's perfect."

My question is, "By whose standard?"

I believe everyone is perfect in the definition of who they are.

For instance, take a clean white sheet of paper. Some people might say it is a perfect clean white sheet of paper.

What happens when you tear it?

Is it now imperfect?

I say, "No." It is now a perfect white sheet of paper with a tear. The definition has just changed.

Wonder if everyone in the world dressed the same, talked the same, had the same hair and skin color, was the same size, had the same personality, remained the same age, ate the same food and the list goes on.

How boring! We'd be like predictable robots. I say, "Viva la difference!"

To me everyone is perfectly who they are. I like to look at people with my spiritual eyes. This is how Jesus looked at everyone. Jesus saw everyone as perfect.

When you look at people with eyes of love, realizing that they are on their own spiritual journey you can see their perfection.

We are made in the image and likeness of God.

I believe this means, you are not your body or your mind. Who you really are is a glorious, vibrant spiritual being having the human experience. You are perfect because your true essence is Love.

Jesus said, "Love your neighbor as yourself."

I think everyone does just that. Unfortunately some people don't love themselves very much.

Your true self is a Loving Being.

Therefore we can say, "Love your neighbor as a Loving Being."

I believe life is about discovering Love. We live in a perfect world of contrast.

People are like mirrors. They teach us who we are and what we don't want to be. When you look at the world with loving, spiritual eyes it is beautiful.

These are the times I like to say, "If this was heaven it would be just fine."

God Is Love

"Not all of us can do great things.
But we can do small things with great love."
~ Mother Teresa

I think my favorite three words in the bible can be found in the book of John, chapter 4 verse 8. "*God is Love*."

I have a plaque hanging on my wall that says, "*God is Love. Therefore if it's not love, it's not God.*"

I think the best solution to any emotional problem is to simply ask the question, "What would Jesus do?" I think it would be the same answer to the question, "What would Love do?"

Jesus is God.

God is Love.

Therefore Jesus is Love.

I wrote a children's song called "God is Love." I'd like to share some of the lyrics with you now.

God is Love
God is perfect Love
He is everything that's good
God is Love
Mother holds her baby tight
Daddy helps me fly my kite
God is Love
People loving others

Sharing with our brothers
God is perfect Love

"I love you," is the most powerful statement in the entire universe.

Never hesitate to say it.

When we say "I love you" and it's unconditional, we are giving love the way God loves us.

When we say "I love you" with no expectation it is a perfect gift.

When we say "I love you" when someone we love is frustrated or angry and saying unkind things we are saying what Jesus would say.

There's nothing more powerful than that!

When someone is shining their love light on you and you do it together you are in perfect harmony with God.

Love makes life beautiful. So shine your spectacular light of love on the world every day.

This is how we create heaven on earth. This is when we say, "If this was heaven it would be just fine!"

God Loves a Good Story

"All these places had their moments
With lovers and friends I still can recall
Some are dead and some are living
In my life I've loved them all"
~ John Lennon and Paul McCartney

I once heard God created man because God loves a good story. I love that.

Life is all about experiencing pain and joy. Although every individual story of how, when or where we experience them are different, the human emotions we all feel are quite the same.

When we are in a state of pain we look for God. When we are experiencing joy we are living the life God intended.

You are living your story. No other human being will ever have the same thoughts or experiences as you. You are a unique, beautiful spirit having the human experience.

Right now think of how you would continue the phrase, "Once upon a time there was a …" and then tell the story of what you are doing right now.

For instance right now I could say something like, "Once upon a time in the great state of Texas, there lived a woman named Cynthia who loved to write about finding heaven on earth."

Wouldn't you love to have journals of the last 7 generations of your family? How about the last 20 or even 100?

My brother has letters my grandfather wrote my grandmother from overseas before he passed away in World War II. They are precious to our family.

I think it's a good idea to write memoirs for your family. Give it to them at Christmas. It would be like gold for the generations to come.

Write about love. Tell stories about funny things that happened to you or something a relative did. How about those challenges you met that had a happy ending. What did you learn from the experience? How did you feel?

How do you want the world to remember you? This is your chance to tell your story and pass it on.

Here's something to get you started. Once upon a time there was.... One day something amazing happened!

You are co-creating your story with God right now. God gave you free will. This means in any moment you can choose what will happen in the next moment.

When you choose love, peace and joy you are living your precious life on earth as it is in heaven. These are the moments of quiet strength when we can honestly say, "If this was heaven it would be just fine!"

My Grandfather, Boder Jordan, “Sport” was granted the Silver Star after spending three and a half years in a Japanese prison camp. He was killed in friendly fire just three weeks before the camp was liberated.

Good Enough?

"Ring the bells that still can ring.
Forget your perfect offering.
There is a crack in everything.
That is how the light gets in."
~Leonard Cohen

Have you ever not done something because you think you are not good enough? That is how I felt for the three years I procrastinated recording my first CD of ambient piano music. I practiced and tweaked and practiced and tweaked until the day I met my friend Jerry Webb at a neighborhood bar in Hendersonville, Tennessee called, "Lower Places." He was playing guitar in a band I had come to listen to.

Jerry had just opened a recording studio.

"I want to record some piano compositions I have created," I told him. Do you have a piano in your studio?"

"I do."

"What kind?"

"I have a K.Kawai."

"That's what I have! It must be a sign."

A month later I was recording my first CD of ambient piano. Three weeks after the CDs were pressed, I had a record deal with Page Music to do 11 CDs of soothing instrumental music. Within three years after my Ave Maria had been number one for several weeks on mp3.com, there were more than 4 million downloads of my piano music I guess I was good enough.

Striving for perfection, I was overwhelmed at first. Finally I figured that if I simply allowed God's love energy to flow through me I could accomplish this task. I put photos of those I loved all over my piano, put my body on automatic pilot and played from my heart, thus creating "musical love energy."

Many times people have commented that they can hear love when they hear my music. This fascinates me. I know I played with Love but when people actually say they can hear it I am amazed. When I was playing with love in my fingers I was playing with God in my fingers.

Now I am writing books. I no longer worry whether or not I am good enough. I simply ask God to help me write what the reader should know. I guess you could say that when I write music and books God is my co-creator.

We are the creative ones of the animal species. Look around you. How much of what you see was manifested from someone's thought?

May I suggest you get started on that dream you have been putting off because you think you are not good enough. Who cares? Those who love you will love it. There is always perfection in what some might deem to be imperfect. Ask any mom with a refrigerator full of their child's drawings.

I am happiest when I am creating. This is my heaven and it is just fine!

Golf

"Golf is a game that is played on a five-inch course - the distance between your ears."
~ Bobby Jones

When our son, Jordan was in the first grade we put him in Little League. Unfortunately he was on the "Charlie Brown" team. After three seasons of almost no wins Jordan became very discouraged and frustrated.

"We never win, Mom. I'm not having fun," he said one evening after a 12 to zero ballgame.

"Why don't you try golf," I said. That's a game where you play all by yourself and you don't have rely on the talent of the rest of your team."

With that, we bought Jordan a set of golf clubs and Dennis taught Jordan how to hit the ball. He began by hitting a bucket of balls from the house to the barn, 400 feet away.

As Jordan grew older he joined the Hendersonville High School golf team in Tennessee. He was named "Golfer of the Year" in his senior year and went to the state competition.

Through the years, when Jordan would leave the house to practice, I would press the palms of my hands together, bow and say, "Ahh little Grasshopper, remember you are the ball, you are the club, you are the hole, you are the field of green grass."

I don't really know why I said it, I just did.

One day, when he was about twelve-years-old Jordan finally looked at me and said, "What does that mean anyway, Mom?"

Sometimes I hear myself say things I don't know I know. It must be God, there's no other explanation. I had the answer!

"What happens when you blow everything up a million times?" I asked. "What do you see?"

"Empty space," he replied.

"Ahh little Grasshopper , it is there you are one with the ball, one with the club, one with the hole and one with the field of green grass."

"Oh. Now I get it," he said with a great big smile. "Bye Mom!"

I sat down in a chair surprised at the insight God had given me. It was amazing.

Jordan had 3 holes in one before he was 21 years old. One of the holes was a par 4 and his Dad was there. Two years later his dad aced the same hole. It was his dad's first hole in one and Jordan was there.

What a gift and at the same time, a strange coincidence.

Ask any golfer and they will certainly tell you a hole-in-one is as close as you can get to perfection and the experience is definitely heaven on earth. If you are a golfer, the next time you hit a hole-in-one and you are dancing around the green remember to say, "If this was heaven it would be just fine!" Especially if it's your first one!

Gone Where?

I am standing upon the seashore.
A ship, at my side
spreads her white sails to the moving breeze
and starts for the blue ocean.
She is an object of beauty and strength.
I stand and watch her
Until, at length, she hangs
like a speck of white cloud
just where the sea and sky come
to mingle with each other.
Then, someone at my side says,
"There, she is gone"
Gone where?
Gone from my sight. That is all.
She is just as large in mast,
hull and spar as she was when she left my side.
And, she is just as able to bear her load
of living freight to her destined port.
Her diminished size is in me -- not in her.
And, just at the moment when someone says,
"There, she is gone,"
there are other eyes watching her coming,
and other voices
ready to take up the glad shout,
"Here she comes!"
(Author unknown)

Grandmothers

Grandmas hold our tiny hands
for just a little while,
but our hearts forever.
~Author Unknown

Sundays have always been special to me. I think it's because when I was a little girl after church we would go to "Moe's" house. Her real name was Sarah and she was my Dad's mother.

Moe used to fix pancakes in a big black iron skillet. She also made delicious hamburgers and apple pies. When Mom would try to cook like Moe she'd always say, "It just doesn't taste the same." Years later I moved to Texas where I learned about country cooking. One day I called my mother and told her I discovered Moe's secret. "It was that seasoned big black iron skillet!" I was so excited.

After breakfast I would beg Moe to play the piano. I wanted to make music so bad and she'd let me play the high notes while she rocked the house singing and playing her honky-tonk tunes. She was AWESOME! My first memory of playing with Moe was standing up. I remember my fingers were just above my eye level. I must have been just a toddler.

Moe had lost her husband in World War II. During the War she raised four children working in ammunition factories and doing laundry during the day. At night she'd play the piano and sing. Moe was awesome! I once saw her hold an audience for over two hours. When she finally got up to take a break everyone moaned and shouted, "Don't stop!"

I started playing the piano and picking out tunes when I was three. I begged for piano lessons and on June 1st 1964, I had my very first lesson. I was ten-years-old.

On my eleventh birthday, my maternal grandmother, Tita, bought me my first piano. Her husband, Pa-pu had passed away. She told me later she bought the piano because of what her beloved husband had said the day I was born. He held up my hand and said, "Look at her long fingers. One day these little hands will play the piano."

Sometimes I wish there really was such a thing as a time machine. I would revisit those moments when I could hear Moe play or I would play for Tita. Now my grandmothers are a beautiful memory alive in my heart.

For many years, when I sit down to play the piano I like to pretend my grandmothers are in the room with me. I always thank them for their beautiful gifts of music when I do.

If you still have your grandmother, savor those moments with her. Tell her you love her. Write down her stories. They will be like gold for generations to come.

If you are a grandmother make beautiful memories for your grandchildren. Mine call me Nana.

I believe grandmothers have the power to create heaven on earth.

I know mine did!

Those wonderful days with Moe and Tita were just like heaven and it was just fine.

My Moe

Happy Birthday to Me

"A Very Merry Un-birthday to you!"
~The Madhatter

It was my 44th birthday. I hadn't heard from any of my three brothers. I knew they were all busy so I figured instead of wondering if they were going to call, I called them. This started a birthday tradition we have done for several years.

This year on my birthday my brothers Kurt and Steve both called. My brother Mark is usually the one who forgets. This year was no exception. About 8pm I called Marky up and when he answered the phone I started singing, "Happy Birthday to me, Happy Birthday to me!"

He said something I thought was brilliant. "I'm so glad I finally caught you!"

We both laughed.

"Mark," I said, "I don't think I ever want you to call me on my birthday. It's more fun this way.

Just because someone doesn't call you on your birthday doesn't mean they don't care about you. I personally don't like to guilt anyone. I think it's a waste of energy. Real love is unconditional. It's the way God loves us.

Every day can be a birthday because every day is an opportunity to give birth to a brand new beginning. This is certainly worth celebrating! If heaven is like a birthday party it will be just fine!

Heaven and Hell

"Hell begins on the day when
God grants us a clear vision
of all that we might have achieved,
of all the gifts which we have wasted,
of all that we might have done
which we did not do"
~ Gian Carlo Menotti

There once was a preacher who was trying to prepare a sermon about heaven and hell for his congregation.

That evening an angel came to him in a dream.

"I have come to show you heaven, and hell," the angel said.

"First I will show you hell."

The angel brought him to a very tall set of beautiful golden doors. Inside there was a spectacular room with a long table full of people. The table was set with a clean white brocaded tablecloth, gold speckled china, golden forks, knives and spoons, elegant lace napkins and the most beautiful flower arrangements you have ever seen. In front of every person at the table was a steaming bowl of delicious soup.

The people around the table all looked miserable. Some were even crying. You see, none of them could bend their arms. They just silently stared at the delicious soup before them. The preacher was amazed. Hell was quite different from anything he had ever imagined.

The angel smiled and said, “Now I will show you heaven!”

The angel brought him to a very tall set of beautiful golden doors. Inside there was a spectacular room with a long table full of people. The table was set with a clean white brocaded tablecloth, gold speckled china, golden forks, knives and spoons, elegant lace napkins and the most beautiful flower arrangements you have ever seen. In front of every person at the table was a steaming bowl of delicious, heavenly soup.

The people in this room also could not bend their arms. Yet everyone was eating, talking and laughing. They were having a wonderful time! So what did the preacher see that was different??The people were all feeding each other! So dear friend, the next time you are invited to share a meal with people you love, may I suggest that if you are giving the Thanksgiving prayer you include, “Thank you God! If this was heaven it would be just fine.”

Heaven

As I sit here by the sea
I think of years gone by
All the good times that I've had
and I breathe a little sigh

I think about my family
the friends that I have found
Some have gone to heaven
and no longer are around

When my life is over
I hope God's house will be
a place like this one I call home
with love and memories

That's why at times you'll find me
when sitting by the sea
Telling God, "If this was heaven
it would be just fine with me!"
~ Duke Jordan

Heaven I'm In Heaven

"Heaven on Earth' is a choice you must make,
not a place you must find."
~Dr. Wayne Dyer

When my daughter was a little girl she had a thing going with a little boy in her class. His name was Wyatt. We lived in rural East Texas where the children all grew up together.

In Kindergarten they used to chase each other every day on the playground.

In the first grade they were in the same class and all through the day they would catch each other looking at the other one.

In the second grade they were in different classes so they only saw each other on the playground and when they did they'd smile.

In the third grade a friend of his came over to Denise in the cafeteria and told her Wyatt wanted her to be his girlfriend. Denise said, "I can't! I don't think my Daddy would like that!"

In the fourth grade, Wyatt sent a note to Denise that said, "Would you be my girlfriend?" The words Yes and No were written on the paper. Denise circled "Yes." That year Wyatt bought Denise a necklace with a golden heart and a pearl on it. She still has it. Denise bought him a San

Francisco 49er ball cap because it was his favorite football team.

Then finally, in the 5th grade someone had a birthday party and Wyatt asked her to dance.

That evening when Denise came home she said, "Mommy, I danced with Wyatt tonight. In my head I was singing, *Heaven, I'm in heaven and my heart beats so that I can hardly speak.*

It was precious. That year we moved to Nashville, Tennessee and the Denise and Wyatt story became a sweet, innocent memory.

I think Denise found her *on earth as it is in heaven* at that birthday party. Although it was the first time they actually touched in all those years their hearts had already found each other back in kindergarten when she was chasing him on the playground.

I hope this story made you smile. I always do when I think about

Heaven, I'm in heaven... and it was just fine.

Heaven Is Not a Rock Concert

"His disciples said to him, 'When will the Kingdom come?' Jesus answered and said, "It will not come by watching for it. It will not be said, 'Look here!' or 'Look there! Rather, the Father's kingdom is spread out upon the earth, and people don't see it!'"
~ Book of Thomas

Have you ever been to a rock or country music concert? Did you ever go backstage? Chances are that if you did, you had to get past a big, burly, intimidating bouncer with great big muscles protruding out from under a very tight shirt. These guys are usually not very friendly and rarely do they smile.

Before you can go backstage, you usually have to show a colored piece of plastic to prove that you qualify to enter and mingle with the stars. Only special people have the privilege to get past his gate and enter the sacred area. If you are not one of the chosen few, you can't get in.

Heaven is not a rock concert. Everyone is welcome. Jesus is the Star and loves you unconditionally. In fact all you have to do is quiet your mind and you're there. There is no qualification or special pass to get in. All you need is to know you are loved and never alone. Heaven is where God is and God is everywhere.

So remember friends, heaven is not a rock concert. You don't have to go through anyone or anything to get to God. You don't have to worry about being worthy or special enough to get close to the Star of the Show. A friendship with God is an intimate, one-on-one, sacred communion that can occur in any moment of your life.

All you need is to be aware.

When I feel the presence of the Holy Spirit it makes my heart full. It is in these times I like to say, "I'm in heaven and it's just fine."

Holistic

"When health is absent wisdom cannot reveal itself, art cannot become manifest, strength cannot be exerted, wealth is useless and reason is powerless."
~ Herophilies, 300 B.C.

Holistic simply means the mind, body and spirit connection.

The Spirit is always good. This is where all the love, knowledge and the complete understanding of our connection to God is.

The mind processes everything. It also has the ability to create, transform and make choices.

The body is a vehicle. It is our physical identity.

When the spirit is enlightened and aware of itself miracles happen. This is where all miracles are created and thoughts and dreams manifest into the physical plain. Just as the violin is to the tree the spirit is to God.

The mind is where we try to define what's real. Sometimes it gets confused and forgets the only thing that is real is love which is synonymous with God.

When the spirit is realized, the mind makes better choices and creates miracles.

When the mind is right the body will let the spiritual light shine through.

The spirit is beautiful.

When the mind sees, hears and makes choices with its spiritual self then the body is beautiful.

If everyone on earth realized they are beautiful, loving spirits with a mind and a body it would be just like heaven and it would be just fine!

Hugs

"I will not play at tug o' war
I'd rather play at hug o' war
Where everyone hugs
Instead of tugs...."
~Shel Silverstein

"Where is heaven?"

"Up there."

"Up where?"

In the book of Luke Jesus says, "The Kingdom of God is within you."

So where is the kingdom of God?

I looked it up. According to most definitions the Kingdom of God is also called The Kingdom of Heaven.

Therefore we can also say, "The kingdom of heaven is within you."

Maybe this means when we are emotionally experiencing love, peace or joy we are experiencing the Kingdom of Heaven.

Jesus also says, "The kingdom of heaven is at hand."

Maybe this means heaven is closer than we think.

To me this is a very comforting thought.

I feel like Jesus is in my heart.

If you agree, then cross your arms over your heart right now and hug yourself.

I like to think that this is how we can give Jesus a great big hug.

If you hug someone else, especially heart to heart, this is another way we can give Jesus a hug. After all Jesus told us that when we do something to anyone else we are doing it to him as well.

When I hug someone I never release first. Some people really need a hug and there are some hugs that will stay in my memory forever. Our daughter, Kristi is famous for her warm strong hugs. It is a beautiful way to transfer love energy and can be a powerful healer.

Here are some great thoughts on hugs from some unknown authors:

"A hug is a handshake from the heart."

"You can't give a hug without getting a hug."

"A hug delights and warms and charms that must be why God gave us arms."

"Hugs are the universal medicine."

"A hug is a great gift - one size fits all, and it's easy to exchange."

"Happiness is an unexpected hug."

"A hug is worth a thousand words."

"Every time I think of you, it is like getting a hug from the inside out. "

"A hug is two hearts wrapped in arms."

"Never wait until tomorrow to hug someone you could hug today."

"Sometimes it's better to put love into hugs than to put it into words".

"A hug is the shortest distance between friends."

"There is nothing like a big Mommy hug!"

"When we hug heart to heart we hug God and we create a beautiful moment of heaven on earth."

So if there is someone you can hug today, for heaven sakes do it! It will be just like heaven and it will be just fine.

I Am the Universe

"I have faith that the universe will be beautiful and simple."
~Einstein

What is prayer exactly? Do you ever feel that praying is a waste of time? After all, God surely knows what we want. Asking for it sometimes seems so futile.

When I gaze upon the vastness of the ocean knowing there is so much more beyond the horizon I am in awe. If a dolphin should appear I begin thinking of whole other world mysteriously blanketed beneath the surface of the sea before me. Again I am in awe. At night, when the horizon blends with the darkness of the sky I look up and see the moon and the stars and think of the trillions of galaxies beyond. Awesome!

So where is God? Is God somewhere I cannot see? Is God beyond the horizon? Is God beyond the moon and the stars? Maybe God is swimming with the dolphins below the surface of the ocean.

Then I remember. God is in all the empty space. God is the conductor of the vast universe that makes music in perfect harmony. I am alive which gives me the privilege to enjoy God's universal song.

Every drop in the ocean creates the ocean. Every star we see creates the Milky Way and every molecule of earth creates that which we call home.

I am the drop… the star… and the molecule; therefore I am the ocean…the galaxies… and the universal song. It is in the empty space I am one with God and all that is.

When I pray I declare my desire. When I listen to God's loving silence I am at peace. Turning my attention to the perfection of nature's harmony reminds me that everything is in perfect order. It is then that I see heaven on earth and everything is just fine.

I Love You Calls

"A sympathetic heart is like a spring of pure water bursting forth from the mountain side."
- Anonymous

"Hi! It's Cindy! This is an, *I love you call!"*

I make *I love you calls* all the time. I do it when someone is on my heart and I just want them to know I am thinking of them.

I do it with friends, my husband, my children and other members of my family.

Maybe I got the idea from Stevie Wonder:

"I just called to say, I love you.
I just called to say how much I care.
I just called to say I love you.
And I mean it from the bottom of my heart."

Sometimes people don't know what to do when someone they know is going through a tough time. *I love you calls* are perfect for this! When my friend, Tamara's mother was in her last days, I left "I love you calls" on her answering machine. She said she listened to them every day and it really helped get her through her sad time.

Now Tamara sends me *I love you calls.*

Saying *I love you* is always a good choice when you don't know what to say to someone when there is stress or sadness.

It's easy to tell people *I love you* when you feel good about them.

It's not so easy to say *I love you* to anyone who has insulted you or violated you in some way. However it can be a powerful tool to begin the healing process. Withholding saying, "*I love you*" intentionally is an illusion of the ego.

Some people need a thimble full of love to say *I love you*. Some need a barrel. Some can't say it at all. When you say *I love you* with unconditional love and no expectations you are giving the gift of love as God gives it. Love is the most powerful energy on earth.

I remember one of my favorite moments when I heard *I love you*. When my grandson Marcus, was three-years-old we went to dinner at an Italian restaurant in Dallas. It was Christmas time. All of a sudden he looked up at me from his plate of spaghetti with those big blue eyes and with a great big sigh he said, "Nana, I just love you so much!"

"I love you too Marcus." I said as I felt my heart dance.

It was a beautiful gift. Everyone at the table just looked at him and then at me and smiled. It was a heavenly moment.

When Marcus says *I love you* it is magic. I get all tingly and as I am savoring the moment I think, "If this was heaven it would be just fine!"

"I just love you so much Nana."

If Texas Was a Woman

"Texas will again lift its head
and stand among the nations.
It ought to do so, for no country upon the globe
can compare with it in natural advantages."
~Sam Houston

I love the way Texans love Texas. A friend of mine once referred to Texas as "God's Country." I think it's amazing how Texans have a pledge of allegiance to Texas and the fact they sing the state song at schools and general meetings.

I was born in California and I have lived in Texas for half my life. I always wanted to write a song that describes "that Texas thing." As a songwriter my challenge was to try to describe the incredible patriotism and love that Texans have for Texas.

One night, as I was driving to a music gig from East Texas to Shreveport it came to me. I would use a metaphor. By the time I arrived to my music gig I had written a song that honors the beautiful qualities of a woman and the Great state of Texas.

If Texas was a woman she'd hold me in her arms
And rock me like a baby close to her heart
If Texas was a woman softly she'd whisper
I will always love you wherever you are

If Texas was a woman I'd marvel at her beauty
Like the colors of a sunset lighting up the western sky
If Texas was a woman she'd sing to me so sweetly
A song that tells her story in a Spanish lullaby

I'd see a billion stars forever in her eyes
Stars that shine like diamonds on a moonless Texas night
If Texas was a woman I know that she would hold
The secret to a love affair that runs deep inside my soul
If Texas was a woman she'd love me deep inside my soul

Now that I have lived in Texas I certainly understand why my friend calls Texas "God's Country." I think Texans especially native Texans would all agree, "If heaven is like Texas, it will be just fine."

If This Was Heaven It Would Be Just Fine

Lyrics by Cynthia Jordan
(Sing to the melody The Water is Wide)

I look across a field of green
To rolling hills and a clear blue stream
The wind is gentle A dove flies by
If this was heaven it would be just fine
Children laughing by the sea
Dolphins dancing with a spirit free
Nature is singing in perfect time
If this was heaven it would be just fine
I am content I feel peace
My soul is singing in harmony
I breathe in deeply the gift of life
If this was heaven it would be just fine
I feel joy within my heart
Blessings are flowing from near and far
All of creation in Love Divine
If this was heaven it would be just fine
I see a rainbow after the rain
My heart is singing I feel no pain
God's great Love like sunlight shines
If this was heaven it would be just fine

In Perfect Harmony

"Always aim at complete harmony
of thought and word and deed.
Always aim at purifying your thoughts
and everything will be well."
~Mahatma Gandhi

In 1971 all of America was singing "I'd like to buy the world a coke." The story of this historical ad campaign is fascinating!

Bill Backer was on his way to Dublin, Ireland to meet with Billy Davis and Roger Cook to write the new Coca Cola commercial. His plane had been detained in London because of heavy fog. The passengers were grumpy and spent the night in the airport.

The next morning he noticed people talking and even laughing with each other. Some of them were drinking cokes.

He was inspired and later said, "I could see and hear a song that treated the whole world as if every person was someone the singer would like to help and get to know."

With that, Backer wrote the line "I'd like to buy the world a Coke" on a napkin and shared it with British hit songwriters Cook and Roger Greenaway.

After he met with his songwriting friends they created the Coke commercial and a legend was born.

"I'd like to buy the world a home
and furnish it with love
Grow apple trees and honey bees,
and snow white turtle doves.
I'd like to teach the world to sing
in perfect harmony
I'd like to buy the world a Coke
and keep it company."

The Seekers recorded the song and it was a big flop with the Coca Cola bottlers. A commercial was shot on the hillside in England but the shoot was ruined with rain and other location problems. Bill believed in his vision and would not give up.

Finally there was enough budget left to shoot the commercial with Roma Films. They recruited Italian volunteers and on a glorious sunny day, on a hillside near Rome, history was made. The commercial featured a group of young people from different cultures lip syncing the song on a hill outside Rome, Italy. The labels on the Coke bottles were in different languages. It first aired in July, 1971. The commercial was magical!

Although Europe had a lukewarm response to the commercial, America embraced it. Thousands of people were calling radio stations requesting the song.

Why? I think we were tired of losing our friends and family in Viet Nam and the idea of a harmonious world resonated with every American heart. Later the New Seekers recorded the song again and it was a huge hit. I believe Jesus would have loved the song. It could have been his theme song! *"I'd like to teach the world to sing in perfect harmony."*

Just think if we lived in a world where everyone shared and cared we'd all be singing, "If this was heaven it would be just fine!"

Invisible

"The greatest treasures are those invisible to the eye but found by the heart."
~Maryanne Williamson

Have you ever thought that the most powerful forces in the world are invisible?

Music is invisible. I have been writing and performing music all of my life and I have witnessed the power of music completely transform an audience.

Thoughts are invisible. Have you ever heard the phrase, "Be careful what you think?" Science has even proven how powerful thought is. Everything created by man began as a thought. It is wise to replace any negative thinking with positive thoughts.

Words are invisible yet very powerful. The first sentence in the book of John says, "In the beginning was the Word, and the Word was with God, and the Word was God."

Energy is invisible. We know the great power of the waves and the wind. Energy defines everything.

Life itself is invisible. Breath is invisible

Love is invisible. Love is absolutely the most powerful force in the universe. It is so powerful it can disarm any weapon of mass destruction!

All of these powerful, invisible forces are within your reach.

If you think good thoughts, say good words, and immerse yourself in the power of Gratitude and Love you will see miracles happen.

Anytime I need to eliminate fear in my life I say, "All is well, Thy will be done." It always brings me peace.

I get quiet and I remember that am I loved and never alone. Then in my bliss I say, "Thank you God! If this was heaven it would be just fine!"

Invitations

"A single conversation with a wise man
is better than ten years of study."
~ Chinese Proverb

When I was a little girl, I loved to get those colorful cards that said, "You Are Invited." It usually meant I was going to a birthday party and this was always exciting.

So many times people say "no" to invitations because they have somehow prejudged the outcome. It seems like sometimes the older people get, they are unwilling to try something unfamiliar or maybe they think the experience is just not worth the effort. I say, trying new things will keep you young and adventurous.

To me, invitations are always an opportunity to experience food I've never tasted, things I've never done and most especially meeting new people.

Just the other day, I talked to a lovely couple with an adorable two-year-old baby girl. They told me they met at an event neither of them really wanted to go to. "I looked at him and thought he was cute," the young woman said with a grin. "Then I looked at his hand and saw he wasn't wearing a ring. Nine months later we were married."

I never prejudge or decline an invitation because I feel it is beneath me or unimportant. This is because I have put God in charge of creating opportunities for me.

Therefore, to me every invitation is an opportunity from God.

Life is precious and there is always something new to experience. If you let go of expectations and see every invitation as an adventure, you will never be disappointed. It's all about attitude, sharing and giving.

When you take the focus off of, "What's in it for me?" and put it on, "What can I do to create joy?" you are thinking like Jesus. Jesus says "yes" to anyone who invites him to their party.

What would your life be like if you lived each day as if you have been invited to a party on earth for just a few hours?

What can you do every day to make the world the joyful place God designed it to be? This is how we can create earth as it is in heaven. I invite you to pick a day and live it as if it were your last. It will be a whole new experience!

You might even see on earth as it is in heaven, and it will be just fine.

Is That God Nana?

"Respect the child.
Wait and see the new product of Nature.
Nature loves analogies, but not repetitions.
Respect the child. Be not too much his parent.
Trespass not on his solitude."
~Ralph Waldo Emerson

Did you know that in many languages the word heaven is the same word for "sky"?

One evening my grandson Marcus and I witnessed a majestic, beautiful sunset in the West Texas sky. The clouds reflected beautiful shades of yellow, orange, pink and indigo. There was a sparkling silver lining framing the top of the cloud.

It was absolutely glorious!

"Is that God, Nana" my little Marcus said with wonder.

I smiled.

"The sunset is a beautiful gift from God to remind us that God is always with us," I answered.

"Oh," he said.

It was a moment I will hold dear for the rest of my life.

I found myself witnessing the sunset through Marcus's bright blue eyes.

Jesus told his apostles, "When you see the world through the eyes of a child you see the kingdom of heaven."

I felt suspended in a timeless moment of peace and joy as we looked at the beautiful masterpiece God had created for us to share.

Jesus said, "The kingdom of heaven is within." I know what Jesus meant because in that moment my heart was overflowing with love and appreciation.

I really felt like I was looking at the kingdom of heaven. Marcus is my joy and we were together in the spirit of awe, love and peace.

"Thank you God for this beautiful sunset you gave us to look at!" I exclaimed.

"You're welcome, Nana," Marcus said with his cherub little face.

Now anytime I witness a sunset I think of that magical moment with Marcus.

"You're welcome, Nana."

Children naturally know their oneness with God because they are fresh from the other side. Sometimes they talk about their "imaginary friend". I think these are ancestors or maybe their guardian angel. Just because we don't see them doesn't mean they're not there.

Right now Marcus is 3 years old and knows what I am remembering. I listen to every word he says. "When we look at the world through the eyes of a child we see the kingdom of heaven."

In time he'll forget.

We all do.

Then on his journey of rediscovery, Nana will be there to help him remember. That's what enlightened grandmothers do.

When we remember and communicate in our oneness with God, it's just like heaven, and it's just fine!

Nana Heaven

It's A Wonderful World

"The great lesson is that the sacred is in the ordinary,
that it is to be found in one's daily life,
in one's neighbors, friends, and family,
in one's back yard."
~Abraham Maslow

The most beautiful train ride I have ever taken was between Florence, Italy and Rome.

I saw so many people, reading, sleeping and talking. They were missing all the beautiful scenery.

I was looking out the window taking it all in.

How many times do we focus on only the destination and miss the journey itself? This is where all the magic is. The journey is where we can appreciate all of God's beautiful gifts.

Life is a journey. Heaven is the destination. A big goal is really the result of the accumulation of achieving smaller goals. Because of this I believe, we can experience the destination in the journey. Or in other words, we can experience heaven in our life's journey.

Wonderful World is one of my favorite songs. I changed one little phrase in the song to illustrate my point. I'd like to share with you now.

I see trees of green, red roses too
I see them bloom for me and you
And I think to myself,
"If this was heaven it would be just fine"
I see skies of blue and clouds of white
The bright blessed day the dark sacred night
And I think to myself,
"If this was heaven it would be just fine"
The colors of the rainbow so pretty in the sky
Are also on the faces of people passing by
I see friends shaking hands saying how do you do
They're really saying I love you
I hear babies cry I watch them grow
They know much more than I'll ever know
And I think to myself,
"If this was heaven it would be just fine"
Yes I think to myself,
"If this was heaven it would be just fine!"

Don't miss the journey. You might miss heaven in our Wonderful World! Jesus said, "The kingdom of heaven is at hand."

I think Jesus would agree, "If our *Wonderful World* was heaven it would be just fine"

Joe and Little Joe

"There is an endless net of threads
throughout the universe...
At every crossing of the threads there is an individual.
And every individual is a crystal bead.
And every crystal bead reflects
Not only the light from every other crystal in the net
But also every other reflection
Throughout the entire universe."
~ Indra's net

I have always said, "Real success is how you make a difference in people's lives." When you hear about something good happening to someone you never met because of something you did, it's really awesome!

I was having coffee with a DJ I had met in Nashville, Tennessee. Her name was Andie, and she had worked at WWWW Radio in Ann Arbor, Michigan. She was excited to learn I wrote the song, *Jose Cuervo*.

"I have a great story about *Jose Cuervo* I want to tell you," she said with enthusiasm. "It's really cool."

"I love *Jose Cuervo* stories!" I told her.

The phone rang at the station one morning and this guy says, "Hi! This is Joe. Can you play *Jose Cuervo* for my son Little Joe so he can sing and dance?"

He was live on the air. "Sure I can! How old is your son??" Andie asked.

"He's seven." Joe answered.

"Hmmm..." Andie said. "That's interesting. You're sure *Jose Cuervo* is one of his favorite songs??"

Joe continued, "Little Joe knows all the words to *Jose Cuervo* and he just loves to sing the song. He even made up a little dance routine."

"Well Ok then," said Andie. "And now we have *Jose Cuervo*, by Shelly West for Little Joe so he can sing and dance!"

This went on for weeks. Every few days Joe would call and request *Jose Cuervo* for Little Joe so he could sing and dance. Andie and Joe would have brief conversations. At one point Joe shared the fact that Little Joe's Mama had died a few months before. He would always say, "The song just makes him happy."

Andie had been receiving his regular calls from Joe requesting *Jose Cuervo* so he and his son could sing and dance. Then all of a sudden several weeks went by where Andie hadn't heard anything from Joe.

Finally one day the phone rang and it was Joe!

"Joe!! Where've you been??" Andie exclaimed. "We've missed you!"

"Things haven't been too good lately," Joe said. "Our house burned down. Can you play *Jose Cuervo* for my son, Little Joe so he can sing and dance! It sure would make him happy."

The listening audience had heard about a man who had lost his wife, and his house had burned down. It was Joe!

Furniture, clothes, money and household necessities showed up for Joe and his son through the radio station.

Friends he had never met were there to help. All because Little Joe loved to sing and dance to *Jose Cuervo.*

Every day we all have the opportunity to touch someone's life in a positive way. When we perform an act of kindness, it acts like a pebble that has been cast into crystal blue, still water. The rippling effect goes on forever and touches people you will never know. This is because we are all connected with the golden thread of God's great love.

The story deeply touched my heart. Just think if everyone in the world was only kind and shared their blessings with others we would have a perfect world.

Earth would be a place where we could all say, "If this was heaven, it would be just fine!"

Jose Cuervo

"Miracles happen every day, change your perception of what a miracle is and you'll see them all around you."
Jon Bon Jovi

All of my life I have loved making music. I have been playing the piano since I was 3 years old. When I was 24 I wrote my very first song. The song was called, *Jose Cuervo*. In 1983 it became Billboard's number one country song of the year.

For years people have asked me how that happened. At first I would tell them the whole story. Now I simply answer, "God."

The story goes something like this: Once upon a time there was a surfer girl named Cindy who lived in California. She loved making music. When she was ten-years-old she begged for piano lessons. For one year she practiced her lessons on the neighbor's piano. Then on her eleventh birthday her grandmother, "Tita" bought her a piano.

After a few years of piano teachers Cindy began to study with Doctor Nino Albanese, an accomplished concert pianist. Eventually Cindy began teaching herself. She loved classical music as well as the Beatles.

One evening Cindy picked up her guitar and wrote her very first song. Her friends loved it. One day after a series of synchronistic events Cindy found herself in the music business. Al Gallico, who was a big time music publisher, heard Cindy's song and brought it to Nashville. Everyone passed so she decided to record it herself. Warner Bros discovered Cindy's record and her version went to number one in Los Angeles but failed to make it anywhere else because the record promoters did not believe in the song.

Cindy was very frustrated. She had worked very hard calling radio stations all over America, showing up at special events and getting press. She was a *has-been* before she even got started.

One afternoon she was in her living room with a very bad attitude. In fact she started yelling at God. "So you can make oceans, mountains and solar systems and I'm supposed to be impressed!" she screamed. "All I want is a little hit song. Is that too difficult for you? You promised if we ask we will receive. I have done everything I can! Why don't *You* do it??" With that Cindy fell on the floor sobbing and completely surrendered.

This is the part where God steps in.

A few months later, Snuff Garrett, who was producing Shelly West brought Cindy's song into her recording session. He was aware *Jose Cuervo* went number one in Los Angeles and thought it would be a good song for Shelly to record.

Steve Dorff the other producer opposed the idea. *As they were disputing whether or not to record it, the piano player, John Hobbs popped up and said, "I was on Cindy's session, I can make a music chart for everyone in five minutes. I like the song."* The rest is history,

That was the magical moment only God knows how to create. Einstein once said, "Coincidence is God being anonymous." Boy was he ever right!

Within two years of my complete surrender my fun little song was Billboard's Song of the Year.

I have learned many things about how God works since the success of my song. Maybe telling you this story now is one reason God allowed it to be successful the *Jose Cuervo* story never ends. I meet people all the time who can sing my song to me. Every time this happens I am amazed!

I thought things like this only happen to special people. I never thought of myself as special. Now I know everyone is. God doesn't have favorites. God's love is equal to all.

Surrender is a beautiful thing. The next time you feel frustrated just turn it over to God. You are never alone and believe me God can do a much better job. If you don't get exactly what you ask for, it only means God has something better for you. This you absolutely *must trust.*

If my record had gone number one I would not have accomplished other things in my life that I am so grateful for. This includes my husband, my children, my ministry, my piano compositions and countless more blessings.

My favorite part of writing *Jose Cuervo* is hearing friends I've never met tell me a story of a happy memory associated with my crazy little song. This is magical to me because I know that somehow I have touched their lives.

For many years I questioned why *Jose Cuervo* was so popular. I realized one day it was never about tequila or waking up next to strange cowboys.

For one thing it's a happy lively song but I think the real magic of the song is in the bridge.

The music is playing – Life is our song

My spirits are high – God is joy and all that's good

Tomorrow might be painful – Contrast and challenges help us to know God

Tonight I'm gonna fly – What would you do right now if you could do anything at all with no restrictions or worry about being judged?

Do you have a dream?

First get proactive.

Then trust God and let the journey unfold.

Savor the journey. It really is the best part.

When we experience God we experience heaven on earth. The thrill of writing a number one country song of the year continues to be an awesome experience. In fact every time I hear other people sing my song it's just like heaven and it is just fine!

Jose Cuervo:

Well it's Sunday morning and the sun is shining
In my eye that is open and my head is spinnin'
Was the life of the party and I can't stop grinnin'
I had too much tequila last night
Jose Cuervo you are a friend of mine
I like to drink you with a little salt and lime
Did I kiss all the cowboys did I shoot out the lights
Did I dance on the bar did I start any fights

Now wait a minute things don't look too familiar
Who is this cowboy sleeping beside me
He's awfully cute how'd I get his shirt on
I had too much tequila last night

All those little shooters how I love to drink them down
C'mon bartender let's have another round
The music is playing my spirits are high
Tomorrow might be painful tonight I'm going to fly
High!!

1983 Cindy Jordan publicity photo

Journey of the Dolphin

"Praying is talking to God.
Meditation is when we listen."

"In the beginning was the word and the word was…' sound." Therefore to get back to the origin of creation, we go to the silence or what some call, the "soundless sound." It is in the silence that we become aware of the space that exists between all matter.

Silence is beyond the speed of light, contains all knowledge and is the cohesive energy that connects all things. The unified field is the origin of all thought and anything we experience in our physical world. Meditation is simply getting into sync with the unified field.

When I try to understand meditation I like to think of when I was a child on the first day of school. I remember the teacher gave me a fresh clean piece of white paper and a brand new box of crayons. I can still smell the crayons. Then she told me to draw a picture. A part of me jumped with excitement because I knew there was no limit to what I could draw on that paper. That is the way I see the unified field. It is the place where anything can happen.

When I first began to meditate I would close my eyes and try to get quiet. I read books, attended lectures and listened to audiotapes to learn the "right" way to meditate. I heard, "Go to the silence and when thoughts come crashing through treat them like smoke and let them wisp away."

I finally found my own personal method of meditation. When I did, I realized there is no real "right way" to meditate because it is a personal and sacred event. First I put on piano music mixed with the sound of waves. I like music with lots of space between the notes. Getting in sync with harmonious energy is very healing. Then I close my eyes and imagine that I am on a wondrous journey with a friendly dolphin. I once heard someone say, "Listening to ocean waves is like listening to God breathing." I loved that. The waves get me I touch with my dolphin friend and the rhythm of my breathing.

I completely trust the dolphin, who acts as my guide as we explore the depths of the ocean. The water is warm and I am quite comfortable. Deeper and deeper we go and all of the turbulence from the outside world soon disappears. Deeper and deeper we go and I stay in a state of continuous anticipation. Finally I fall into the calmness of what the depth of the ocean has to offer.

Meditation is a wonderful way to heal the mind and the body through our spiritual connection with God. Through the meditation process the body can re-organize itself and create a healthy state of being. Beautiful music, the peaceful sounds found in nature or an imaginary dolphin friend can make a world of difference on your mystical journey called life.

For me meditation is simply celebrating my oneness with God. Wherever we find God we find heaven and all is well.

Kitchens

"But our waking life, and our growing years,
were for the most part spent in the kitchen,
and until we married, or moved away
it was the common room we shared. "
~ Laurie Lee

Mothers are the heart of the family and the kitchen is the heart of the home. Our kitchen is the room in the house where family and friends bond. We make the morning coffee, bake birthday cakes, dance, create fabulous meals and play games in the kitchen.

I see my kitchen as a fun place to be. I don't "slave in the kitchen", I play in the kitchen. When I was a little girl I loved to play house. I would make a pretend sink, stove and table out of cardboard boxes. Now when I'm in my kitchen and I want to make it fun I just pretend I am a little girl again only now I am using real stuff.

In all three homes that we've shared, my kitchen floors have always had a space big enough for dancing. My husband and I have been known to spontaneously dance in the kitchen any time of day or night when we hear certain songs. I also promote dancing and singing while doing dishes. Again, I like to make it fun.

Kitchens are magical. Did you know the sense of smell can evoke an instant memory? I can especially remember the smell of my Grandmother's kitchen on

Sunday mornings. Moe would make us buttermilk pancakes with crisp lacey edges.

Years later when I first met my husband's mother I walked into her kitchen and tears came to my eyes. Grannie's kitchen smelled just like Moe's. This makes perfect sense. They were both experts at down home country cooking. My Dad has told me when he goes to heaven, he hopes Moe will meet him there and present him with her apple pie. "No one makes an apple pie like she did," he likes to say.

My dear friend, Karen, invited me to her home for a small luncheon one afternoon. I remember the table cloth was beautiful and vanilla scented candles were softly burning on the table.

"Karen, is this your china?" I asked. "Yes and my good silver as well," she answered.

"I feel special!" I said.

Karen told me something I will never forget. "Why would I save my crystal, my fine silverware or my good china for special occasions or someone special coming to dinner? Who is more special than my family and friends? These are the people I love."

What an awesome thing to say. I have since taken on her attitude.

I think Thanksgiving is my favorite meal of the year. My husband always cooks a delicious Thanksgiving dinner and I especially like his cornbread sage dressing. Our table is usually filled with family and friends and the meal is spectacular. Every Thanksgiving I always think, "We should have more than one Thanksgiving dinner a year."

You can create heaven on earth in your kitchen every day if you want to. I like my kitchen to smell like love with something baking or cooking on the stove.

Don't let these good years pass you by especially if you have children at home. You can anchor to love by creating smells they will always remember. Now that we are empty-nesting, I so appreciate when any of our children are in my kitchen eating with us.

Nowadays I never take time with loved ones for granted. My kitchen is used for cooking, baking, dining, dancing, playing games and celebrating with people I love.

The kitchen is the heart of my home. This is because the food is prepared with love and nourishment for the people I love most.

Loving your kitchen is a simple matter of attitude and perception.

Next time you are preparing and sharing a meal in your kitchen with people you love, take a moment to really savor the experience with gratitude and appreciation. Your soul will dance with delight.

If there are kitchens like mine in heaven, heaven will be just fine.

Let Me Be There

"Music is the mediator between the spiritual
and the sensual life."
~ Ludwig van Beethoven

Uplifting music with a message of love and joy is always good for the soul. To me it is the best medicine in the world.

In 1973 Olivia Newton John recorded and released a song written by John Rostill called *Let Me Be There*. I have always loved the song and one day as I was listening to it I had a thought: what a perfect song for Jesus to sing! Just imagine Jesus singing these words to you.

Wherever you go
Wherever you may wander in your life
Surely you know
I always want to be there
Holding your hand
And standing by to catch you when you fall
Seeing you through
In everything you do

Let me be there in your morning
Let me be there in you night
Let me change whatever's wrong and make it right
Let me take you through that wonderland

That only two can share
All I ask you is let me be there
Watching you grow
And going through the changes in your life
That's how I know
I always want to be there
Whenever you feel you need a friend to lean on,
here I am
Whenever you call, you know I'll be there

In 1985 I moved to East Texas and joined a small church in Waskom, Texas. The church had a piano but no one played. Naturally I became the music minister and enjoyed my position for twelve years.

I had always picked songs with good messages to sing at church. Once in a while I would have the congregation sing a song that most people knew but were not found in the hymn books. Right now I can see the smiles and the joy on the people in that little church singing *Let Me Be There.* It's a beautiful memory.

I imagine Jesus loved music. I wonder if he liked to sing. I bet he had a beautiful, gentle voice when he did...

Can you think of songs that have an uplifting message?

Listen to them.

Sing them. When we experience music with our heart, the soul dances with heavenly delight and proclaims, "If this was heaven it would be just fine!"

This is my grandparents' wedding photo.
The day I was born my grandfather said,
"One day those fingers will play the piano!"
Tita bought me my first piano. I am grateful!

Lord Teach Us to Pray

"One day Jesus was praying in a certain place.
When he finished, one of his disciples said to him,
"Lord, teach us to pray, just as John taught his disciples."
~Luke 11:1

The following is a direct translation of *The Lord's Prayer* from the Aramaic language to English.

"Oh Thou, from whom the breath of life comes,
Who fills all realms of sound, light and vibration.
May Your light be experienced in my utmost holiest.
Your Heavenly Domain approaches.
Let Your will come true - in the universe (all that vibrates)
just as on earth (that is material and dense).
Give us understanding, assistance for our daily need,
Detach the fetters of faults that bind us,
like we let go the guilt of others.
Let us not be lost in superficial things but let us be freed
from that what keeps us off from our true purpose.
From you comes the all-working will,
the lively strength to act,
the song that beautifies all
and renews itself from age to age.
Sealed in trust, faith and truth.
(I confirm with my entire being)

My very favorite part is, "*Let your will come true in the universe just as on earth.*

I believe God's will for humanity is to walk in harmony in the spirit of love, joy and peace. I think Jesus would probably agree. I'll bet if he was on earth right now he might say something like, "Just love each other. Then earth will be just like heaven and it will be just fine."

Love says…

Ego is simply an idea of who you are
that you carry around with you.
~Wayne Dyer

When ego says, "I am right."
Love says, "Help me understand you."

When ego says, "You are mine."
Love says, "I love you."

When ego says, "It is expected."
Love says, "It is appreciated."

When ego says, "I am my things."
Love says, "I am Love."

When ego says, "I am better than …"
Love says, "I am equal to all."

When ego says, "Nobody is perfect."
Love says, "Everyone is perfect."

When ego says, "I am having a bad day.
Love says, "All days are good."

When ego says, "I don't care."
Love says, "We are one in Spirit."
When ego says, "I am afraid."
Love says, "God is always with me."

When ego says, "You make me happy."
Love says, "Happiness is found within."

When ego says, "I am alone."
Love says, "I am all things."

Ego says, "I will never forgive you!!"
Love says, "I forgive you as Jesus forgave from the cross."

Heaven is when we look at the world through eyes of love and when we do it's just fine!

Charlie with his big brother Cameron

Love Your Enemies?

"It has been my misfortune to be engaged in more battles than any other general on the other side of the Atlantic; but there was never a time during my command when I would not have chosen some settlement by reason rather than the sword." ~ General Ulysses S. Grant

Jesus said, "*Love your enemies.*"

"Are you kidding??"

He also said, "*Do not resist an evil person. If someone slaps you on the right cheek, offer the other cheek also.*"

"No way! Come on!"

I think Jesus was talking about the power of surrender.

"What??" you say.

The best day of the Civil War was April 12th 1865. That was the day General Lee surrendered to General Grant at the Appomattox Court House in Virginia and the Civil War was finally over. That was the day the soldiers could go home and America was reborn with the opportunity to again be the *United States*.

There were one and a half million casualties in the American Civil War. As I see it both sides lost.

Both sides felt God was on their side.

Wayne Dyer says, "When you have the option to be right or be kind, kind is always the best choice."

I have learned this to be true.

Making friends is so much better than making enemies. When we violate because we have been violated we are equal to that which has violated us.

One hundred percent of the time, when someone violates you, it really has nothing to do with you personally. Something bad has probably happened to them or they are part of an unenlightened group. Happy people who like themselves and love their life don't hurt others.

When my daughter was in Middle School there was a young man who waited at her locker every day and was relentless at tormenting her. One day she came home upset and told me about him. "Tell me something to tell him, Mom!"

Next time you see him say, "I really feel sorry for you. Someone must be treating you mean for you to be so mean to me."

He never bothered her again. In fact, when he'd see her at school he would say, "I'm OK, I'm OK!"

She completely disarmed him with compassion. Compassion is an act of love. She felt empowered. This is because love is the most powerful energy in the universe. It can even disarm the atomic bomb!

Compassion and forgiveness are acts of love. God is love. Therefore compassion and forgiveness are acts of God and there's nothing more powerful than that!

So be compassionate and forgive your enemies. Don't worry. You don't have to invite them to dinner or anything. Just love them. It will eliminate the darkness and bring peace to your heart.

There is only love in heaven. There are no enemies at all.

God loves every single human being equally.

Jesus saw that light of God's love in everyone.

Look at people with your spiritual eyes. These are the eyes of love. These are the eyes of Jesus.

Advocate love, not war. It is empowering.

When you do you will see heaven on earth. In moments where I feel all things are possible and I experience the light of God in another human being I always say to myself, "If this was heaven it would be just fine!"

Mary and Martha

Women wish to be loved without a why or a wherefore;
not because they are pretty, or good, or well-bred,
or graceful, or intelligent, but because they are themselves.
~Henri Frederic Amiel

In 1988 I was living in East Texas. The local cable station agreed to do three episodes of a children's Christian show I created called, Let's Celebrate! As part of the show we decided to go to a school and interview small children with different questions.

One of the questions we asked was, "What would you do if Jesus was going to come to your house."

A little 5-year-old girl named Linzie Solomon had the cutest answer. She had dark sparkling eyes and a big red bow on her long dark curls. Linzie smiled, folded her hands, nodded her head and said, "I would invite him to have a tea party with me!"

What would you do if you knew Jesus was coming to visit you tomorrow?

Would you try to make your home perfectly clean?

What would you serve?

One of my favorite stories in the New Testament is in the Gospel of Luke.

Now as Jesus and his disciples went on their way, he entered a village, where a woman named Martha welcomed

Jesus into her home. She had a sister named Mary, who sat at his feet and listened to what he was saying.

But Martha was distracted by all of the things she felt like she had to do. She came to him and asked, "Lord, do you not care that my sister has left me to do all the work by myself? Tell her to help me!"

Jesus said, "Martha, Martha, you are worried and upset about many things but only one thing is important. Mary has chosen the better part and it will not be taken away from her."

No wonder women who knew Jesus loved him so much. He saw them as important.

Maybe Jesus also said something like, “Martha. Why don’t you get out of the kitchen for now and sit with your sister Mary and me. All of that can wait until later. In fact I’ll help you.”

I think this story has a lot of insight to how we see our priorities. Can you imagine how awesome it would be to have Jesus come to your house!

I know I wouldn’t be in the kitchen. I would serve something very simple and hang on to every word he had to say.

Then as we did dishes together we would certainly sing and make it fun and say, “If this was heaven it would be just fine!”

Merrily Merrily

The supreme happiness of life
is the conviction that we are loved.
~Victor Hugo

Have you ever heard the phrase, "The grass is greener on the other side?"

Where is your heaven on earth? Where is that sacred, special place where you feel peace, love and joy?

I know for my son he likes to go fishing.

For me it's sitting in the warm sun on the sand In Redondo Beach, California, where I grew up, watching the waves gently break on the sand.

I asked a little girl one time to tell me about heaven. She said, "Heaven is where dreams come true."

I just loved that.

Children have the spiritual wisdom that we have forgotten. They come to this world with the understanding that "dreams really do come true." This is because they come straight from heaven and know all things are possible with God.

Let's look at the wisdom of a song I learned in kindergarten.

Row Row Row your boat
Gently down the stream.
Merrily Merrily Merrily Merrily
Life is but a dream

Row Row Row your boat –
You have the free will to make choices and to be proactive on life's journey.

Gently down the stream –
Let go and let God.

Merrily Merrily Merrily Merrily –
God created this beautiful earth for us to be happy.

Life is but a dream –
God is all that is real

As the little girl said, "Heaven is where dreams come true."

Remember the next time you feel "Merrily Merrily, Merrily Merrily," give thanks to God and say, "If this was heaven it would be just fine!"

Motherhood

"When you are a mother,
you are never really alone in your thoughts.
A mother always has to think twice,
once for herself and once for her child."
~Sophia Loren

Being pregnant was one of the most beautiful experiences of my life. Every day I had a craving for peanut butter, mayonnaise, lettuce and dill pickles on toasted wheat bread. That was my part. God took care of the rest.

About four months into it I could feel my baby moving inside. This was magical. I love being a woman and I feel blessed that I have known what it is to have the miracle of life growing inside of me.

I always smile at pregnant women. There is a silent knowing that all mothers have. You don't even have to say a word. The smile says, "I really do know what you're going through and it's beautiful."

Although I talked to my children and played music for them before they were born I didn't really meet them until I first held them in my arms. All three times I said, "Hello. I am your Mommy and I'm going to take care of you."

I think my favorite experience of being a new mother and probably my lifetime was feeding my babies the natural way. Nourishing my little baby in the way God designed a woman to do was absolutely the greatest satisfaction I've had as a woman. Watching their little mouth move and hearing their sweet grunts and sighs gave me a peace and sense of importance I have never known.

I think if I could pick any moment in my life to go back to, it would be the experience of being a new mother feeding my little baby. The quiet contentment, the sound, the trust, the smell, and the warmth of their little bodies were truly my greatest time as a woman.

Now the experience only exists in a beautiful memory. If you are a new mommy, next time you hold your sweet little baby in your arms give thanks to God for your precious blessing. Savor every moment. It will be a memory soon enough.

Then as you reflect on the miracle you are participating in say, "Thank you God. If this was heaven it would be just fine."

Denise and little Sarah

New Beginnings

"We live in a wonderful world that is
full of beauty, charm and adventure.
There is no end to the adventures we can have
if only we seek them with our eyes open."
-Jawaharial Nehru

Do you remember your first day in school?

I remember mine!

I remember new kids, new shoes and my pretty teacher Mrs. Tabor. She looked like a movie star and had a big beautiful smile.

Mrs. Tabor gave each of us a clean white sheet of paper and a brand new box of crayons.

Wow!

I can still smell those crayons.

What should I draw??

The possibilities are endless! What color crayon should I pick??

This is so exciting!!

Wow!

What should I draw?

Do you remember a moment like that?

God gave us free will. This means that in any moment you have the power to choose what will happen in the next moment.

Just like that brand new white blank piece of paper, the possibilities are absolutely endless.

This is very exciting.

Every moment is a new beginning.

Here's a little spiritual exercise for you to try. For five minutes imagine that you are a being from another planet who just popped into your body to see what it's like to be a human being. You only have a short time to experience what it's like to hear, see, taste, smell and touch.

What would you do different?

Now imagine you only have five minutes to live.

What would you do different?

These are great spiritual exercises I like to do to get in touch with the beautiful gift of life and appreciate God's blessings.

Do this every day and I promise your blessings will multiply. This is because appreciation vibrates at the highest level.

If God told you to draw your greatest happiness on that white, clean piece of paper what color crayon would you pick? What would you draw??

Happiness is a choice. An attitude of gratitude is good place to start.

What is it that fills your heart with peace, joy and love?

Right now, picture your happiness in your mind. I see my grandson Marcus. In fact I always tell him, "You are my happiness."

May I suggest that today, in a moment of happiness, show God your appreciation and say, "Thank you God!

Thank you for my happiness. If this was heaven it would be just fine." It will make you feel good. It will make you feel God.

Think of a joyful moment and write it here:

Nothing

"You may say I'm a dreamer
But I'm not the only one.
I hope someday you'll join us
And the world will live as one."
~ John Lennon

The following riddle was presented to a group of five-year-old children. They answered it correctly.

What is greater than God, worse than the devil, Rich people need it, Poor people have it and if you eat it you will die?

Now think a minute

What is greater than God, worse than the devil, Rich people need it Poor people have it and if you eat it you will die?

Let me give you a clue.

Simply answer the first question.

What is greater than God?

Of course!

Nothing!

Let's break that down.

No-thing is greater than God!

So what is the No-thing?

The No-thing is the blank canvass. It is silence before the music.

It is the beautiful place from which all things are created. Everything you see, feel, touch, hear and smell was created from the No-thing.

It is exciting to me to be aware of the unlimited potential we have when we co-create with God. God makes the flowers and we make the garden. God makes the trees and we create the house and numerous other things. God gives us water and we make a swimming pool.

Look around you right now. If you are inside you are probably looking at something that was manifested from God's beautiful gift of imagination. This is what makes us different from all of the other living things on earth. If you are outside in nature you are probably looking at many of God's beautiful gifts created for us to enjoy.

In the book of Malachi it is written, "I the Lord do not change." I believe God is the *only* thing that never changes. Everything else has the potential to be transformed into something else. This includes our attitude. This is why I know we can change the world into a wonderful place of total harmony.

When we experience God we experience Love.

When we experience Love we experience God.

Just think of what kind of a world we could co-create with God's *Love* energy. We absolutely have the power to do this because all things are possible with God.

All we have to do is go back to the no-thing. Just think of it as a blank canvass where only good is allowed. Think of only loving words and beautiful music are created from the silence.

The next time you feel that beautiful emotion of love with a child, a friend or even your dog, be grateful and say “Thank you God.” It is from this place we can create a new world full of love and harmony.

Let’s dream it together and change the world! It can be just like heaven and it’ll be just fine!

Our National Anthem

"Let us trust God, and our better judgment
United we stand, divided we fall.
Let us not split into factions
which must destroy that union
upon which our existence hangs."
~Patrick Henry

If you have ever been to an NFL or college football game you have probably had this experience.

You are at the ball game maybe even dressed in the colors of your team. The air is full of excitement and the spirit of "winning". Thousands of people are filling up the stadium. In the seats across the field from you are fans wearing the colors of the opposite team. They are clearly "the enemy".

Suddenly everything becomes quiet and together, the whole stadium focuses on the American flag. For many, especially those who have served or have family in the military, their hearts are full of pride and emotion, as they watch the red, white and blue colors gently wave in the breeze.

For two precious minutes, thousands of people experience the power of unity as they sing the National Anthem.

O say can you see by the dawn's early light
What so proudly we hail by the twilight's last gleaming

Who's broad stripes and bright stars
through the perilous fight
O'er the ramparts we watched were so gallantly streaming
And the rockets red glare the bombs bursting in air
Gave proof through the night that our flag was still there
Oh say does that star spangled banner yet wave
O'er the land of the free and the home of the brave

Then, as soon as the music stops there is usually a huge cheer and it feels good. The coin is tossed and the magic is gone. Division and competition has once again set in and the game begins.

I love the National Anthem. Just think of the millions who have sung these lyrics over the years. Think of the young soldiers who sang it on foreign soil and what it meant to them as they reflected on their homeland and the families who loved them.

Music is so powerful. Singing our National Anthem always moves me to tears. If I get to experience emotions like these in heaven, heaven will be just fine.

People Just Can't See It

"When Jesus spoke again to the people, he said, "I am the light of the world. Whoever follows me will never walk in darkness, but will have the light of life."
~ John 8:12

When Jesus taught us to pray he said, "Thy kingdom come thy will be done on earth as it is in heaven."

It was January 18th 2003. My daughter Denise had had an accident and was on life support. I learned later her doctor had told the nurses to call when it was over.

God gave us a miracle that day. I'll never forget the first thing my daughter Denise said to me when she woke up from her coma. She was only seventeen and the words she said changed my life forever. It was so beautiful I quickly wrote them down so I wouldn't forget.

"O Mama! I saw the most beautiful light. All I could do is look at it. I had no thoughts. It was so beautiful there are no words that can even describe it. There was only love and I couldn't stop looking at it. It felt like a warm blanket of only love wrapped around me. Mommy, the light is all around us, people just can't see it."

As she spoke to me her eyes were filled with light. It was 3 o'clock in the morning. Her doctor didn't expect her to ever wake up again. It was because of this experience I have learned to completely trust God. I have the complete knowing that all things are possible with God.

Some people might say what Denise experienced was only a dream. I know a few people who have had similar experiences. Most of them keep it to themselves because it is so sacred and a reaction of disbelief saddens them.

I for one like to make people feel safe to share their beautiful story and I have heard some good ones. Some floated over their bodies. Others saw a tunnel of bright light and saw loved ones who have passed on. One man I know was touched by and actually heard the rustling sound of an angel's wing. All of them expressed a feeling of peace like nothing they ever experienced before.

I think we can all agree that God is always with us. We are never alone. The peace in that hospital room as Denise told me about her journey to the light was like no other I have ever experienced in my lifetime.

Now, anytime I am with my Denise, I am reminded of her beautiful words. "Mommy, the light is all around us, people just can't see it."

Maybe heaven is closer than we think. Maybe it is right here now.

I've heard it said, "Heaven is the place where God dwells." Therefore it makes sense heaven is on earth in a dimension most of us cannot see. However, when I close my eyes and quiet my mind I know I can feel the loving touch of God. That in itself is the mystery of faith.

God has greatly blessed those who have seen the glorious light and can share that experience with those of us not so fortunate.

And "God bless those who have not seen yet still believe."

Heavenly Light shining so bright
Beautiful light of his love
Wonderful light shining so bright
Glorious light of his love
Love everywhere Jesus is near
Wonderful light of his love
Glow through the earth give us new birth
Beautiful light of his love
Jesus the glorious light of the world
Jesus the wonderful light of the world
There is love all around
There is love all around
With Jesus the beautiful light of the world
~Cynthia Jordan

"The light is all around us Mama. People just can't see it!" When Denise said those words it changed my life forever. I could feel the heavenly light in that hospital room and it was just fine.

Note: My awesome cousin Danny passed away on July 7, 2015. A week before he passed, as the medical team was anxiously trying to revive him with a ventilator, he saw the same glorious light Denise saw. He told his wife Phyllis it was beautiful, sparkly and full of love.

Poo Poo People

"You gotta accentuate the positive
Eliminate the negative
Latch onto the affirmative
Don't ask for Mister In-between"
~ Johnny Mercer

Bobby Bare has a great song called "Numbers." It is based on the idea that there are some men who like to say, "There ain't no tens." The meaning…there is no such thing as the perfect woman.

Hmmm.

The song tells the story of a beautiful girl who walks into a bar and the gentleman singing the song gives her a possible eight and the two of them could make eighteen if her head's on straight.

The young beautiful girl decides to turn the tables around. "You give me an eight well that's a generous thing to do. Now let's see just how much I give you!"

Unfortunately poor ol' Bobby ends up rating a two.

I love this woman's attitude.

It was a Thursday evening. I had been asked to play the piano at a bookstore opening. I decided it might be fun to watch people watch me or I should say, look at *Cynthia the musician.* It was like watching a movie, but I am one of the characters.

By the end of the evening I surmised that there were four different types of people who reacted to *Cynthia the musician*. I only played the piano. I put the characters in the room into four different categories.

The first group I call "Advocates" or "A team" for short. These people were friendly, complimentary, kind and some even eagerly bought my music and had me sign autographs. I like these people.

The second group I call "The Equalizers." They want to make sure that you know you are not better than they are. If you've done it, they have done it too or know someone who has. They are competitive in nature and are not satisfied with who they are. This is clear by the amount of useless information they are feeding you. People who have or have done usually don't have to tell the world. They just know it.

The third group are the "Poo Poo People." They are just plain toxic and rude. Their actions are obnoxious and sometimes hateful. These are miserable people. Give them no energy. Just simply forgive them for, "they know not what they do."

Finally the fourth group I like to refer to as the "Silent Majority." They might not approach you but they have the potential to be any of the other three.

We only let the Advocates in our sacred space. With equalizers you can smile but do not reveal your secrets when they ask. Being mysterious drives them crazy.

Poo Poo People must be avoided like a steamy smelly product left by a great big dog on the sidewalk. Do not step on it! Their emotional disease is quite contagious. Their invisible stink will go with you and you are vulnerable to becoming one of them. Forgiveness is the best solution. It will keep you clean and fresh just like a good rain washing away the muddy filth. In fact when a Poo Poo People says something toxic to you, the best thing you can say is, "I forgive you for that." It will completely disarm them.

As far as the silent majority, be friendly but the last thing you ever want to say to them is, "What do you think." It doesn't matter what they think and it will appear that you are insecure. Be patient. Eventually they will identify themselves.

Heaven is full of the "A Team." There are angels and advocates everywhere because it is the place where only Love exists. If you want to experience heaven on earth spend your time with people who love and appreciate you. That is when we are "on earth as it is in heaven" and all is well.

Prayer of St. Francis

"Lord, grant me the strength
to accept the things I cannot change,
the courage to change the things I can,
and the wisdom to know the difference."
~ Saint Francis of Assisi

I believe one of the most memorable movies I have ever seen is Brother Sun Sister Moon. It is the story of Saint Francis of Assisi, a holy man who lived in the 13th Century.

Francis walked away from his family's wealth to live a life of prayer and poverty. He founded an order of monks and lived in the hills of Assisi helping the poor. Today Saint Francis is known as the patron Saint of animals.

I have been to Assisi, Italy and I must say it was magical. No words can possibly describe the deep feelings of peace I experienced while visiting the tomb of Saint Francis.

The prayer of Saint Francis has been recited and sung for hundreds of years. I believe it is one of the most beautiful writings of all times.

Lord, make me an instrument of your peace
Where there is hatred, let me sow love.
Where there is injury, pardon.
Where there is doubt, faith.
Where there is despair, hope.

Where there is darkness, light.
Where there is sadness, joy.
O Divine Master,
Grant that I may not so much seek to be consoled,
as to console;
To be understood, as to understand;
To be loved, as to love.
For it is in giving that we receive.
It is in pardoning that we are pardoned,
And it is in dying that we are born to Eternal Life.
Amen.

The first part of the prayer speaks in terms of a world full of contrast. Saint Francis reminds us that by using the power of love we have the power to transfer darkness to light. Then he goes on to help us to remember we are one with everyone. When we perform an act of kindness we do it for the good of all.

Just as the caterpillar changes into a butterfly, I believe when Saint Francis speaks of dying he is really speaking of being born again. This can happen in any moment of your life because every moment has the potential to be a new beginning. All you have to do is die to the past.

I found these quotes from Saint Francis I'd like to share with you

"What we are looking for is what is looking.

"All the darkness of the world cannot extinguish the light of a small candle.

"When you are proclaiming peace with your lips, be careful to have it even more fully in your heart.

"Keep trying to do what is necessary, then what's possible and suddenly you're doing the impossible.

"True progress quietly and persistently moves along without notice.

"Remember that when you leave this earth, you can take with you nothing that you have received--only what you have given.

"He who works with his hands and his head and his heart is an artist.

"A real friend is someone who walks in when the rest of the world walks out.

"Take the opportunity to give silent blessings or a kind word to people you see today who need to know they are not alone.

"Recognize your moments of giving as opportunities from God. This will give you the feeling of spiritual joy and grace. Then thank God for the opportunity."

I really love this guy! That feel- good feeling of bringing joy to someone's day makes me think of how we can create heaven on earth by doing at least one act of kindness. I believe that feel-good feeling can be contagious…

I believe that feel-good feeling can make us feel, if this was heaven it would be just fine.

A Recipe for Dreams

"A dream is a wish your heart makes
When you're fast asleep
In dreams you lose your heartaches
Whatever you wish for, you keep
Have faith in your dreams and someday
Your rainbow will come smiling thru
No matter how your heart is grieving
If you keep on believing
the dream that you wish will come true"
~ Disney's Cinderella

A little girl once told me," Heaven is where dreams come true." I used to think that kind of thing happens to other people. Now I know anyone can do it. In fact dream-making is not only possible it's fun! Here are ten steps that work for me.

1. Identify precisely what it is you want to accomplish and write it down. Then put it where you can see it every day.

2. Turn it over to God where all things are possible with God.

3. Create the mantra "Thank you God for (your dream)" as if it has already happened. Say it often every day.

4. Delete any negative thought that it can't happen and replace it with a positive one.

5. Look at every invitation as an opportunity.

6. Look for signs. Be alert and pay attention.
7. Don't prejudge. Blessings can be disguised.
8. Be consistent.
9. See every coincidence as a gift from God.
10. Don't quit! Never give up.

Sometimes you might feel like you're running with your shoelaces tied together. That's a good thing. You might fall, but at least you're moving forward. As long as God is leading your team, you cannot fail. In fact, it's impossible to fail.

The best part of making dreams come true is the journey itself. You don't want to miss a thing. I remember one time a good friend of mine was jumping up and down with excitement when I picked him up from a recording studio in Nashville. "Wait till you hear this! It's so cool!"

We then put a song he had just recorded in the CD player. He was ecstatic. I told him, "Dan, this is the IT you are looking for in the music business. It doesn't get better than this. You can never be happier or more ecstatic than you are in this moment. A cut, a Grammy, a number one song…the euphoria feels exactly the same. Savor this moment and make it last as long as you can."

When a dream comes true it's magical. If you have a dream, for heaven sakes go for it! Give thanks for every accomplishment and tell God you appreciate the help. These are the times I like to say, "If this was heaven it would be just fine."

Sabrina

"Of all the wonderful things
in the wonderful universe of God,
nothing seems to me more surprising
than the planting of a seed in the blank earth
and the result thereof."
~ Julie Moir Messervy

I have a special friend in my life. Her name is Sabrina. I met Sabrina when she was ten years old. Her mother had brought her by our ranch in East Texas to sell me Girl Scout Cookies.

Sabrina was a part of our family and was like a sister to my children. She sang like an angel and I used her on the Let's Celebrate CD project for children. She also participated in the Kids for Kids ministry. I love her like my own.

Several months after Sabrina was married, she came to visit me in Tennessee with a heavy heart.

"I can't get pregnant," she said.

I prayed to God to speak through me.

"Sabrina, you will not be the same mother your mother was to you. She did the best she could do under the circumstances. It's time to forgive her."

I took her by the hand and we walked to the lake in my backyard. We sat on the grass and I began to speak.

"All of the plants and trees you see along the lake came from a seed and grew as one of God's creations. There is a little soul who has already picked you to be its mother. Let's ask God to create the perfect conditions in your body to allow a new baby to grow." With that I put my hand on her tummy and gave her a blessing.

When I pray, I like to light candles with my intention in mind. The flame always makes me think, "God is taking care of it." It always brings me peace.

We then went into the house and lit green candles for fertility. "Dear God, we know there is a little soul with you now that has chosen Sabrina to be its mother. Thank you, God, for making her body ready for a new baby."

A peaceful knowing came over us and somehow I knew everything was going to be OK.

Then I looked at Sabrina and said, "Now I want to be the second person you tell after you tell your husband you are pregnant. He needs to be the first."

I remember this all happened on March 17th which is St. Patrick's Day. The first week in May I was sitting on a swing in my backyard, looking at the lake, when my phone rang.

"Hi Miss Cindy," I heard one of the sweetest voices in the world say.

"Well, hey Sabrina!" I really wasn't expecting what I heard next.

"You told me to call you, Miss Cindy. I'm pregnant. I'm going to have a baby."

Sabrina had a beautiful baby boy she calls Nathan. He also sings like an angel. We will always remember that day. It was a spiritual exchange between two women that still resonates deep inside my soul.

Sabrina is a beautiful, loving mother and I thank God for her friendship and love. I know that when Sabrina looks at Nathan her heart is full. Children are always a blessing. Nathan is a good little singer as well. I am sure when she hears him sing the songs she sang as a little girl Sabrina would agree, if this was heaven it would be just fine.

Sanctuary

A poem by Duke Jordan

When things at work disintegrate
And I feel all alone
I know the pain will always pass
As soon as I get home

When I go out to face the world
No matter where I roam
My daily task seem easier
For I know I can go home

When I go home and say hello
I hear your sweet reply
I find my world is right again
All my troubles pass me by

And when we cuddle on the couch
And I say how much I care
And put my arms around you
And kiss your graying hair

You speak to me so lovingly
In your soft and tender tone
I settle in your sweet caress
And know that I am home

Santa Claus

"Happiness is when what you think, what you say, and what you do are in harmony.
~ Mahatma Gandhi"

My son Jordan is always curious and thinks things through before he presents a question he needs answered.

It was two weeks before Christmas and we were in our kitchen in Hendersonville, Tennessee. Jordan was about twelve years old.

Earlier that year I had been visiting my oldest daughter, Julie, who lived in France. It was Easter and unfortunately their dad wasn't plugged in well enough to remember the Easter Bunny. No chocolate bunnies, eggs or jelly beans showed up. What happened to the magic bunny in the full moon? It was devastating.

The kids expressed genuine concern. At twelve and thirteen they quickly figured out that the Easter Bunny only shows up if Mom's around. To this day if any of my children are home you can be sure the Easter Bunny is probably going to show up.

Apparently Jordan was concerned that maybe Santa Claus was going to pull a "no show" as well.

It was December and I was in the kitchen cooking dinner when Jordan walked in.

"I just can't wait for Santa Claus to show up this year, Mom. I love Santa Claus! He always brings me cool presents. I just can't wait!"

I smiled. Pretty clever I thought. I knew Jordan knew the real deal. After all he was growing armpit hair. I guessed it was time to set the record straight.

"Jordan," I said. "There are three stages of Santa Claus."

"The first stage is for small children. You hear the story about elves, the North Pole, reindeer and coming down the chimney. It's a beautiful story and a wonderful tradition."

"The second stage, you learn that the story of Santa Claus is different than was first presented. You learn that Santa Claus represents the spirit of Christmas and you develop your own ideas about Santa."

"The third stage, you are Santa Claus."

"Don't worry son. I am sure there will be presents from Santa."

As I thought about what I said it occurred to me, these are the same three stages we experience on our spiritual journey.

First, we hear the story of God. Different cultures hear different stories. I think all major religions pretty much agree that God is our Creator and Love is the greatest power on earth.

Second, we process that story. I was raised in a Christian environment so my understanding of God is based on the teachings of Jesus Christ. For me this is simply the understanding that love is always the best solution.

Third, we have a complete understanding of our oneness with God and we live our lives in harmony with nature and our fellow man.

When I hear "Santa Claus" I see a friendly, jolly, roly-poly man with a full white beard, glasses, black boots, and a red and white, furry suit and hat. He is defined in my heart and I have loved him since I was a little girl. This makes him real.

I know I will meet Santa Claus in heaven and I will know him just as I did when I sat on his knee at Sears. He will look at me like he did then and say, "Ho ho ho! Welcome to heaven Cindy! Have you been a good girl? This is heaven where you can be a little girl again and believe in me. I've been waiting for you."

When I sat on his knee it was heaven on earth.

Yes, Jordan, there is a Santa.

If every day in heaven were just like Christmas it would be just fine.

Shadows in the Sand

~ Cynthia Jordan

As I walk towards the waves the sun on my back
I look down and see my shadow
My legs are long and I seem so tall
And I wonder where the time goes
From being a child, a sister, a wife
A mother, a friend different times in my life
I was holding someone's hand
In the shadows in the sand

I see the shadow of little girl
With a man so big and strong
He walked me to the shoreline
Singing a happy song

We played tag with the waves
As they came on the shore
My pigtails flying free
I was holding my daddy's hand
In the shadow in the sand

The only girl with three little brothers
We had a lot of fun
Surfing on our canvass mats
And playing in the sun
Mom would bring a lunch down
The memories are quite grand
I can still see the four of us running to the waves
In the shadows in the sand

In my teenage years my shadow changed
A womanly shape was there
My figure was like an hour glass
And the breeze blew my long hair
A young man with a surfboard
My first love held my hand
I watched as we walked to the shoreline
In the shadows in the sand

Again my shadow made a change
My belly was like a ball
For months I watched her daddy surf
Then she was born in the fall
Now a little girl was by my side
Her pigtails flying free

I held my daughter's hand
In the shadow in the sand
Nowadays I walk to the waves
With the sun upon my back
I realize my shadow has changed
But what sees it never has
Although it looks like no one is there
I know I'm not alone
For now I hold God's loving hand
In the shadow in the sand

Shoe Skates

"You make every game a life and death proposition,
you're going to have problems.
For one thing, you'll be dead a lot."
- Dean Smith

Sometimes life gives you lessons you might not understand at the time. Then one day… driving down the road… you suddenly remember… then a light comes on… and you get it! When I was growing up, there was a girl across the street named Jenny. One Christmas Santa Claus brought both Jenny and I a brand new set of white shoe skates. The city had just poured a new sidewalk in our neighborhood and I learned to skate.

One day I was leisurely skating down the sidewalk when all of a sudden from nowhere, Jenny zoomed by me yelling, "Beat you to the corner!"

When she got to the end of the street, she turned around and started waving her arms, shouting, "I win, I win, I win!"

I was mad. It wasn't fair! I didn't even have a chance.

"Ha, Ha I won," she laughed and then skated away.

A few days later it happened again!

"Beat you to the corner!" she yelled as she raced by.

Again when she reached the corner she started waving her arms yelling, "I win, I win, I win!"

This time I just kind of looked at her trying to figure out what she was so happy about?

Sure enough a day or so later it happened again! She came from behind and challenged me to a race to the corner.

"Ha, Ha, I win, I win, I win!" she shouted with glee.

This time I looked at Jenny and said, "I don't care."

She never did it again.

I found my bliss. At 8-years-old I figured out that Jenny Barretta couldn't win if I didn't get in the race.

In God's eyes, No one is better than you and you are not better than anyone else.

Be happy for people when they reach a goal. If they do it unfairly, that's not for you to worry about. God takes care of that kind of thing and hopefully at some point they will see the light.

The only person you should compete with is "who you were yesterday." When I want to accomplish something I partner up with God. This is because all things are possible with God.

Then when we reach that goal together I say, "Thank You, God. You are awesome. If this was heaven it would be just fine!"

Silence

"A seed while growing makes no sound
A tree when falling makes huge noise
Destruction shouts
Creation is always quiet.
This is the Power of Silence!"
~Syed Imarn

Until my brother-in-law Danny was four-years-old he hardly ever spoke. Finally one day at the breakfast table, Danny said something!

"My eggs are cold," he said with his big brown eyes full of disappointment.

"O my gosh!" his Mama said. "Danny can talk! How come you've never spoken before?"

"I guess everything's been alright 'til now Mama," he responded.

This story of Danny reminds me of a TV show about a talking Palomino that was on when I was a little girl. It was called *Mr. Ed* and the only person the horse would speak to was a man named Wilbur. Mr. Ed was very wise and full of advice for Wilbur. In the theme song of the show there was a line that said, "*People yakkity yak in the streets and waste the time of day, but Mr. Ed will never speak unless he has something to say.*"

I guess that describes Danny. I know so many people who talk, talk, talk more than they listen. I say, "The voice of God is silent. God is all knowing. Therefore if you want to be perceived as, or get in touch with, the *all-knowing*, be silent."

I once heard, "Praying is when we talk to God. Meditation is when we listen."

This makes perfect sense to me. Meditation is when we listen to the beautiful silent voice of God.

I hear frustrated people say all the time, I pray and I pray and I pray and I pray and I pray… Most of these people tend to talk a lot anyway.

I always tell them, "Maybe you should get quiet and listen. God already knows your deepest desires."

When I listen for the silent voice of God I find the eye of the hurricane, the oneness with love, the peace deep within my heart. I hear solutions and become more aware of the gift of life itself. It is in this sacred communion that I feel as if I am sharing the same breath with God's divine spirit.

Some people are uncomfortable with silence. I think the most secure, loving feeling you can have with anyone is the ability to share the quiet. If you love them it can evoke a beautiful feeling of contentment.

It is said, "Words are silver. Silence is golden."

Silence is God's voice. Be quiet and listen for the voice. You'll know it is God if it speaks with love. For me, it comes in the form of thought that I know is not mine and gently says, "I love you and I am always with you." Sometimes the mind gets in the way but the soul always recognizes and understands God's loving message.

I once heard someone say that music is really the silence between the notes. This is why when I play the piano

I suspend the space between the notes so I can hear the voice of God singing.

Next time you are searching for answers, quiet your mind. Beautiful instrumental music can help. Just listen for God's voice in the space between the notes and know you are loved.

Then as you find yourself resonating with the harmonic vibrations of the music, close your eyes and say, "I love you too God. If this was heaven, it would be just fine."

Some Kind of Herb

"Sittin'on the dock of the bay, waistin time"
~ Steve Cropper

One of the interesting things about living in Nashville, Tennessee you never know who you might see about town. One day I saw Johnny Cash at Sam's standing in line in front of me. He was chasing his little blonde, curly haired grandson around the register. I shook his hand and said, "Hi, my name is Cindy. Don't worry, I already know who you are!" I would have probably lost my cool if he had said, "Helloooo, I'm Johnny Cash."

Johnny Cash was a singer-songwriter and a lovely gentleman. "I have a daughter named Cindy," he said with a smile. "Your name will be easy to remember." Now I regret not telling him I wrote *Jose Cuervo*. I am sure he would have loved that.

It's fun being a songwriter because people don't know who you are and when they learn you wrote a song they know well, they always get excited. Some people even sing *Jose Cuervo* back to me.

It was Christmas and my friend Angel Cropper invited our family over for a celebration. My husband and I knew Angel's family when we lived in East Texas. She had gone to Nashville to be a singer where she met her husband Steve Cropper. Steve would later say it was love at first sight! He had never seen a woman hit a golf ball like that before!

At one point my son Jordan walked over and said, "Mom, Steve has written some really cool songs! He wrote *Midnight Hour, Sitting on the Dock of the Bay* and another one about some kind of herb.

"Green Onions?" I asked.

"Yeah, that's it! I've never heard it before."

Steve overheard our conversation and said, "Jordan if you have never heard *Green Onions,* I will give you a hundred thousand dollars!"

"Sure!" he said. "I know you're good for it."

With that Steve Cropper played a version of *Green Onions* recorded live at Oakland Stadium. He took great delight as Jordan was totally surprised and kept repeating, "O my God! O my God!" Steve loved it!

This says a lot about Steve Cropper. All those years of living as the *Green Onions* songwriter and he still got such a kick of watching Jordan completely get excited. (If you haven't heard the song Google it. You will surely know it.)

Steve told us how they had recorded *Green Onions* and didn't know what to call it. The song is played on an organ and Steve plays guitar. It has no lyrics. After the recording someone said, "It stinks like onions!"

Steve said, "My Pappy always liked green onions on the table. Let's call it that!"

This experience with Steve Cropper and Jordan goes down as a moment I would choose to relive in heaven. Listening to a famous song with the songwriter present was just like heaven and it was just fine!

Song Titles

God is Love ~1 John 4:8

Because I am a songwriter I am tuned into lyrics of songs. I thought it would be fun to take the word "Love" in titles of songs and replace it with God.

I found 12 songs where it worked well.

1 .*Make You Feel My God* (Bob Dylan)
2. *God Is a Many Splendored Thing* (Frank Sinatra)
3. I feel it in my fingers I feel it in my toes *God Is All Around* me and so the feeling grows. (Troggs)
4. Shine on the world shine on me *God Is the Answer* (Dan Seals)
5. *God Will Turn You Around* (Kenny Rogers)
6. What the World Needs Now is *God* Sweet *God.* (Dionne Warwick)
7. *God Will Keep Us Together* (Captain and Tennille)
8. Sometimes I am frightened but I'm ready to learn *The Power of God* (Celine Dion)
9. That's the story of, that's *The Glory of God* (Bette Miller)
10. *All You Need is God* (Beatles)
11. *All for God* (Bryan Adams)
12. You get the *Best of my God* (Eagles)

Wherever we find *Love* we find *God.*

We also have the opportunity to know *God* in the loss of someone we love. I think this was best expressed by Alfred Lord Tennyson in 1850 when he wrote, *"'Tis better to have loved and lost, than never to have loved at all."*

Love is the most powerful force in the universe. Of course it is because *God is Love*.

Think of someone right now who you love so much it makes your heart want to burst into a big flame of sparkling light. It can even be a pet. This is your blessing and a wonderful way to experience God.

Be grateful for this blessing. Knowing this experience is your love song. You will be together in heaven as you experienced that love on earth. They are the best part of your story. If they are still with you, treasure every moment you are with them. They are your heaven on earth.

This is why when I feel big bursts of love I like to say, "If this was heaven it would be just fine."

Soul Song

"Oh Shenandoah, I long to see you,
Away you rolling river.
Oh Shenandoah, I long to see you,
Away, I'm bound away,
Across the wide Missouri."
~ Folk song written 19th Century

We were visiting family in Cape Cod, sitting on a porch drinking our morning coffee and gazing at the sea. Out of the clear blue my sister-in-law Janet said, "I love the song *Shenandoah*. I don't know why I love it so much, I just do."

As she spoke her eyes seemed to reveal some kind of soulful memory hidden deep within.

"Then it must be your soul song," I replied.

"My what?" she said, breaking from her momentary trance.

"It's your soul song," I repeated. "A soul song is music that makes you feel what you can't put into words. It just makes you feel."

Janet smiled. "Yeah, I guess you could say *Shenandoah* is my soul song."

"It's funny about that song," I said. "It's kind of haunting. I used to close every show with *Shenandoah* when I was singing in Shreveport. I call songs like that *magic songs*."

We looked up the origin of the song. It is speculated to have been written and sung during the time of the Civil War. The Shenandoah River and valley were named by early Irish settlers because the landscape reminded them so much of the Shannon River in their homeland of Ireland.

There are songs that seem to reach through the sands of time and haunt me in a way that cannot be explained. I also love *Shenandoah* and feel the same as Janet. I don't know why I love it, I just do. The melody can bring me to tears and touches my soul very deeply. When I sing it, I can see a bend in the river in my mind even though I have never actually really been there.

Maybe it's a song of our ancestors. Janet and I both have Irish running through our veins. Maybe it speaks to us from another lifetime faded into the memory only God and the soul is aware of. Is there a piece of music that awakens your soul and creates emotions you cannot explain?

God communicates to us through emotion and music is the language of emotion. I love it when I sing or play a song and people say they get goose bumps. To me this is the part of us where we are one with God coming forth and revealing itself.

After our coffee, I sat at Janet's piano and played *Shenandoah* several times for her. She loved it and it seemed to bond us like soul sisters. As I played her soul song for her, Janet stood by the piano, smiled and said, "You know Cindy, if this was heaven it would be just fine." I loved that.

Strawberries

"There are only two kinds of people
in the end:
those who say to God, 'Thy will be done,'
and those to whom God says, in the end,
'Thy will be done."
~ C.S. Lewis

Once there were three small strawberry gardens that were planted in three separate rooms.

In the first room the strawberry plants were watered and given plenty of sunlight. Beautiful, red healthy strawberries grew on the plants and they were tasty and sweet.

In the second room, the strawberry plants were watered and given plenty of sunlight. In this room a prayer was said every day over the strawberries. "Dear Lord, Please let these strawberries grow as big as plums!" Sure enough, the beautiful, red strawberries grew as big as plums and they were tasty and sweet."

In the third room, the strawberry plants were watered and given plenty of sunlight. In this room, every day, four words were said over the strawberries. "Thy will be done."

The strawberries grew as big as peaches and they were bright red, juicy and delicious!"

Have you ever wondered if you are praying correctly? I know I have.

When Jesus was asked, "Teach us to pray," Jesus taught us the perfect prayer. "Thy kingdom come, Thy will be done."

God already knows our deepest desires and God will always give the best outcome. Just like a good parent, God knows what is best for our spiritual growth. This does not always align with what we want. Just remember through it all, God loves you so much!

When you say, "Thy Will be done," you are telling God you totally trust whatever happens. God knows what's best for your soul. That which brings us closer to knowing God is always the greatest outcome.

Your prayers will always be answered. Be patient and know everything is on God's time.

In the meantime count your blessings and be thankful. I am sure God appreciates appreciation. Appreciation and gratitude are the highest vibration in the universe and acts as a magnet to more blessings.

Then, when you are feeling the joy from your blessings, look to the heavens and shout, "Thank you God! If this is like heaven it will be just fine!"

God will hear you and smile.

Sunrise in New Hampshire

"He who binds to himself a joy
Does the winged life destroy;
But he who kisses the joy as it flies
Lives in eternity's sunrise"
~William Blake

It was a warm September morning 2011 in New Hampshire. I peeked out the window and saw the beginning of one of the most beautiful sunrises I have ever seen in my lifetime. I woke up my husband and ran downstairs.

From the back porch of the farm house we could see a huge bright green meadow with forest trees lining up on both sides. It was a few days after the Autumn Equinox and the trees had begun their transformation to bright orange, red and yellow.

Beyond the meadow were layers of rolling hills. A giant mist flowed throughout the baseline like a blanket holding some kind of mysterious thought.

Behind the tallest hill a warm golden glow was barely lighting up the sky. It was the first light of dawn. I ran up the stairs and grabbed my camera. I knew we were in for a spectacular show!

The clouds were a dark indigo and resembled a fleecy kind of texture spreading throughout the New England sky. In every new minute, the golden ball of light revealed more of herself, turning the wooly clouds soft shades of pink and orange.

There is something about a beautiful sunrise that connects me with my Creator. The sunrise speaks to me in terms of new beginnings and the promise of a timely, consistent presence that only gives.

As I gazed upon the quiet beauty of the morning, my heart was full and my soul was dancing with delight. With each subtle change I felt the sunrise had a divine, personal message just for me.

In a timeless moment I felt God's beautiful silent voice saying, "This sunrise is my gift to you. As you watch its beauty remember, like the sun I will always come when you need me.

I will never let you down. I am here to bring light to your darkness and warmth when you feel cold. I will nourish you and comfort you.

When the day is over it will only seem like I have left you. In the darkness the moon reflects the sun's light. This will remind you that I am right around the bend just a few hours away. When there is no moon, know I am with you in the stars and trust that I am on my way like millions of days before.

Most of all know that I LOVE YOU."

Of course as we quietly watched the spectacular vision unfold, my husband and I made the comment several times, "If this was heaven it would be just fine!"

Taylor Swift

All you need to do to be my friend is like me.
~ Taylor Swift

When my son Jordan was just a baby my friends would actually debate over who got to hold him. He loved to snuggle and would inch up like a little puppy dog with anyone who would hold him.

Jordan went to Hendersonville High School, a city just north of Nashville in Tennessee. About a week before his graduation I remember walking with him through the hallways to pick up his cap and gown. Every kind of kid you could think of was waving at him and some even ran up to hug him. "This is my Mom," he would say. Jordan would then tell me how each of them had touched his life. It was always complimentary and they all walked away a little happier.

This has always seemed to be Jordan's purpose in life. One day when he was still in diapers he looked up at me and said, "Mama when I grow up I'm going to make people laugh." He's been making people smile ever since.

Your integrity and genuine regard for others is *always* in your control. In every moment you have the choice on how to treat people and what to say to them. I like the way Wayne Dyer says, "Always choose *kind.*" Not too long ago Jordan shared a story with me that I think really illustrates why it is so important that we be kind to *everyone*.

Taylor Swift also went to Hendersonville High School. She was a few years younger than Jordan. Jordan had a couple of "buddies" who played hockey in the arena close to the Parthenon in Nashville, Tennessee. One was AJ and the other was a boy named Drew. Jordan and Taylor along with a group of friends would go to the hockey games to support their friends on the hockey team.

Every year at Hendersonville High the school puts on a talent show. Taylor had been in the show and played a song she had written called *Tears on My Guitar*.

Here are the lyrics to the first verse:

Drew looks at me, I fake a smile so he won't see
That I want and I'm needing everything that we should be
I'll bet she's beautiful, that girl he talks about
And she's got everything that I have to live without

Needless to say she poured her sweet little heart out all over the stage. The "Drew" she talks about was one of Jordan's friends on the hockey team. It takes a lot of courage to be a songwriter. Sometimes we share our most intimate secrets with the world. Taylor did just that when she sang her song at the high school talent show.

Jordan heard some smirks and unkind things said by some "mean people." It bothered him because he really liked Taylor.

That next weekend in the lobby of the hockey arena Jordan yelled as loud as he could so everyone could hear, "Taylor! You were awesome at the talent show. I really like your song and you sing really well."

She ran across the lobby and gave him a big hug. "Thank you Jordan! I really appreciate that!"

A few years later, shortly after we moved to San Angelo, Texas, Jordan came in one day and said he had heard Taylor's song on the radio. He was so excited.

"Mom, I heard a friend of mine *sing* a song she sang in the talent show at school. I'm really happy for her!"

Of course now the world knows Taylor Swift. She has become a huge hit. I believe it is because she is determined, radiates a genuine love for her fans and appreciates all her blessings. I have watched her interviews and I have read articles about her. She remains humble and in awe of her success. I love that about her.

Just last week on the Grammys I heard her sing another song called, "*Mean*." The lyrics are :

And I can see you years from now in a bar, talking over a football game
With that same big loud opinion but nobody's listening
Washed up and ranting about the same old bitter things
Drunk and grumbling on about how I can't sing
But all you are is mean

Do you think Taylor remembers everyone who was mean to her? Of course she does. I read in an interview, she doesn't hold a grudge and is very forgiving. But I bet she still remembers.

Do you think she remembers Jordan telling her he thinks she is amazing? Of course she does. The compliment came before she was famous. He told me she is one of the sweetest girls he's ever met.

How do you want people to remember you??

Taylor Swift and my son Jordan experienced on earth as it is in heaven when she hugged him in appreciation for his compliment. When we perform, receive or witness acts of kindness it's just like heaven and it is just fine!

Jordan

Children are miracles and our greatest teachers.

Thank You God

*"For the LORD God is a sun and shield:
the LORD will give grace and glory: no good thing will he withhold from them that walk uprightly. O LORD of hosts, blessed is the man that trusteth in thee.(Psalm 84:11, 12)*

I hear so many people say, "I hope it works" when they pray.

What do you mean I hope it works? Name one thing God cannot do.

I was at the Los Angeles Airport. My daughter Julie was in Italy ready to give birth any minute. My flight was at 8am. I was on standby so I arrived at 5:30 that morning.

About an hour before the flight a big screen started flashing, "Flight Full." I absolutely had to get on that flight! If I didn't arrive in New York by 5 Eastern Time I would have to wait until the following day. By then it might be too late.

I had a small piece of rose quartz in my pocket. I call it my Gratuity Stone. I pulled it out and held it tight and started saying, "Thank you God for putting me on this flight. Thank you God for putting me on this flight."

I heard an announcement, "If anyone will give up their seat to New York we will give you a flight anywhere in the United States."

"Thank you God for putting me on this flight. Thank you God for putting me on this flight."

About 10 minutes later another announcement, "We will give a first class ticket to anywhere in the United States to anyone will give up their seat on the 8 am flight to New York."

I would not allow the slightest doubt to enter my mind! I continued my mantra. "Thank you God for putting me on this flight. Thank you God for putting me on this flight."

I watched as every passenger hand over their precious
ticket.

"Thank you God for putting me on this flight. Thank you God for putting me on this flight."

I saw the big steel doors shut, Boom!

"Thank you God for putting me on this flight. Thank you God for putting me on this flight."

It was 5 minutes to 8. Someone had not shown up. All of a sudden I heard my name! They took me through the door the crew goes through.

As I made my way to the one empty seat on that plane I kept kissing my ticket while saying, "Thank you God for putting me on this flight. Thank you God for putting me on this flight." It made people smile.

It was my miracle, especially designed for me. I believe it happened so I could share the story with you now. After all, what in the world is it that God cannot do?

I made it in time. As they wheeled him out of the delivery room he grabbed my finger as if to say, "I knew you'd be here Nana. Glad to meet you."

Later, I was peacefully holding little Marcus in my arms. I remember thinking, "Thank you God. If this was heaven it would be just fine!"

Julie with Marcus

The Awareness Game

"All the world is a stage.
All the men and women are merely players.
They have their exits and their entrances
and one man in his time will wear many hats."
~William Shakespeare

How many parts have you played in your lifetime? I tried to write all of mine down once and I couldn't finish. I've been the baby, a sister, a wife, mother, waitress, piano teacher, customer, entertainer, friend and the list goes on!

Right now what part are you playing? How would you describe your character? What is the setting?

You have the power in every moment to create your story. The field of potentiality is wide open for you to make choices. You can watch television, pet the dog, bake a cake, drive your car, call a friend and so on. You are the star of your life.

I like to play what I call *The Awareness Game* with my friends and family. I describe the moment at hand as if it is already a memory.

I played *The Awareness Game* with my daughter, Denise, as we were experiencing a dinner cruise. "Remember the time I came out to visit you in New Orleans and we took a Riverboat Dinner Cruise on the Mississippi? You were wearing the new dress I bought you in the French

Quarter and we listened to The Dukes of New Orleans Dixieland Band."

We were creating a memorable story and describing it in the moment seemed to give us more appreciation and even enhance the experience.

Our story took place on a red and white riverboat, cruising on the Mississippi River. The backdrop was a beautiful, orange and golden sunset behind the skyline of New Orleans. I was playing the role of mother, Denise was the daughter.

The characters in our story were servers, musicians, a boat crew and passengers. Everyone on the boat was experiencing their own personal memory and Denise and I were characters in their story. I was also playing the role of customer, fellow passenger and part of the music audience.

God gave us free will. In every moment you have the power to make choices in creating your story.

Sometimes we play several parts at once. What roles will you play today?

Friend? Parent? Sibling? Customer? Boss? Student?

Knowing that God feels your emotions and hears your thoughts, what kind of character will you be?

Happy? Sad? Kind? Helpful? Loving?

You might like to try my little "Awareness Game". It can really be fun I like to think of life as a drama production. Your body is really just a shell that you can decorate any way you want. Your mind is the writer and director and your spirit is the audience, watching and feeling the emotions as you participate in the symphony of life.

Being aware can bring you directly in touch with the *now,* as a spiritual being having the human experience. Living with awareness can give you a profound appreciation for the precious gift of life itself. If you are with someone you can start off by saying, "Remember the time we…?" and then describe the moment at hand.

You always have the power to create your story. We do this with the choices we make. Make God your co-creator and it can be magical. Actually, we are creating a story together now. I am playing the part of author and you are the reader. To me, this is exciting because I am sharing a part of myself with you.

Happiness is a choice. If you focus on those things that make you happy you will find heaven on earth. God can transform anything to good because God is Love.

In these happy moments you might even say, "Thank you God for this precious gift of life and all of the blessings you give to me every day. If this was heaven, it would be just fine!"

The Beatles!

"Here comes the sun and it's alright"
~The Beatles

I remember where I was, that fateful day Ed Sullivan introduced the Beatles for the first time on his show. I was ten-years-old and we were visiting the Welton family. There were eight baby boomer kids and four adults. The adults were all commenting on the long hair and the radical style of music.

"You like them??" Mr. Welton asked like there was something wrong with me.

"Yeah!!" I exclaimed with enthusiasm. "I love them!"

I remember my parents bought me the *Meet the Beatles* album for my birthday and I wore it out. As my life's journey brought me from childhood to young womanhood, I was listening to the Beatles. They were my expression of change. I watched Beatle cartoons every Saturday morning and collected Beatle cards. They used to call it *Beatlemania.*

As I was changing, the Beatles music and writing was changing as well. Their style went from rock and roll to poetry. *I Wanna Hold Your Hand* from their early days was quite different than the song *Imagine* that was written years later.

Last night I went to a Beatle Concert. Some people might say, "That's impossible!" The Beatles broke up over

40 years ago and George Harrison and John Lennon aren't even alive. However, spiritually speaking, I learned that ***yes***, the Beatles are alive and well!

The concert was held at a club on the Redondo Beach pier in California and it was packed full of baby boomers dancing and singing Beatle songs. They were being performed by a young band singing and playing our memories. The first set they were dressed in suits and had "Beatle haircuts." The second set they were dressed like the *Sergeant Pepper* album and then finally the last time out they were dressed casual and "John" had long hair and little glasses.

It was like stepping back into time. The music was the same and the spirit of the music was the same. The only thing different were the physical forms of the baby boomer audience and of course, the performers. Even their dialogue was performed in a Liverpool accent to reinforce the ambience of the act.

My girlfriend Anita and I sang just about every song. The memories were flowing and the joy was contagious. People were smiling and acting just as they did forty years ago. Some had a little less hair and some had a little more weight but the youthful glow and smiles on the faces of the baby boomers were timeless. Everyone there had a mutual knowing of a time shared. Trying to explain it cannot even be put into words. The music seemed to erase all time and in that musical experience many of us were young teenagers once again. It was awesome! Music has the power to break down the walls of time just like a magic time machine. When I listen to the Beatles with my eyes closed I am young again.

I remember one night when living in Nashville, my daughters talked me into going out with them. We went to a club that had four different music venues. While the kids spent the evening dancing to *their music* I wandered into a piano bar where I enjoyed music I was more familiar with.

A young man sat next to me and started a conversation about music. "Do you like the Beatles?" he asked.

"I love the Beatles!" I said with enthusiasm.

"My mom likes the Beatles!" he said with a great big grin. "Who is your favorite Beatle?"

I suddenly realized that I had grown-up. My answer was different than it was when I was a teenager.

"Whoah!" I said. "When I was young all of my friends and I agreed that Paul was the favorite because he was so cute and we liked the way he nodded his head. Now I would say it is John Lennon because he is the one I would love to have a conversation with… Wow!"

Today I would say I don't have a favorite. John, Paul, George and Ringo are one musical genius. Every component was part of the whole. As a musician I especially appreciate George because of his musical genius in bringing John and Paul's music to life with his brilliant musical riffs. These are those familiar musical combinations of notes that make you know what song it is before the first word is even sung.

It has only been a short time in human history that music can be recorded and reproduced as if you are in the room with the musicians and singers. This is quite a gift. Music is a wonderful way to recapture the essence of time that has passed. It can evoke emotions of joy that can lift the spirit into a youthful state of consciousness.

I witnessed this last night at the Beatle Concert. Every baby boomer there seemed to be in a suspended state of timelessness and there was a smile on every face I saw. Anita was my best friend in high school and treated me to *the Beatle* experience last night. Annie Habits and Roland Agular from our class were also there. Last night we were kids again as we sang every Beatle song they played. We were so happy and it was so much fun!

Now I know I can experience heaven on earth with my high school friends and Beatle music. "Anita," I yelled as we were singing, *She Loves You Yeah Yeah Yeah*, "If this was heaven it would be just fine!"

In My Life

~ John Lennon and Paul McCartney

There are places I remember
All my life, though some have changed
Some forever not for better
Some have gone and some remain
All these places have their moments
With lovers and friends I still can recall
Some are dead and some are living
In my life I've loved them all
But of all these friends and lovers
There is no one compares with you
And these memories lose their meaning
When I think of love as something new
Though I know I'll never lose affection
For people and things that went before
I know I'll often stop and think about them
In my life I love you more

The Black Scribble

"Remember how in that communion only,
beholding beauty with the eye of the mind,
he will be enabled to bring forth, not images of beauty,
but realities and bringing forth and nourishing true virtue
to become the friend of God and be immortal,
if mortal man may." -Plato

If you saw your toddler drawing a big black scribble on your clean white wall would you think it was beautiful? Let me tell you about the day my son Jordan did just that.

I had to borrow my neighbor's old green clunker to take my children to the dentist. Mine was in the shop and I was a little desperate because it took months to get an appointment with this particular dentist. The car was smelly and the ceiling was falling down. Nevertheless, I put my two toddlers, Denise and Jordan in their car seats and took off to town.

About 15 miles down the road I saw smoke coming from the hood. I pulled over, got out of the car and knocked on the door of a nearby home to use the phone, (This happened before cell phones.) Thank God no one answered. I looked at the car and more smoke was coming out of the hood.

I ran to the car and saw my sweet babies in the back seat smiling at me. Denise had locked the door but I had the key in my hand. This was another, "Thank God!"

I grabbed both babies and ran. In less than a minute there was a huge booming sound and the car blew up. The old green clunker was on fire, popping and burning black smoke. My heart was racing and I was shaking with fear. Several cars had pulled over to help. One was a neighbor I'd never met named Karen. To this day I call her my angel. She rescued us and drove us home.

I walked down the hallway and saw the black scribble Jordan had created that morning. What if I had to see it knowing I would never see my baby again? I kneeled on the floor and with grateful tears, I kissed the beautiful black scribble and hugged the wall.

I never did clean up that black scribble the whole time we lived in that house. Every time I saw his little drawing it reminded me that our guardian angels are always with us.

To me that black scribble was a beautiful work of art. In fact, if I ever see a black scribble like that in heaven, it will be just fine!

The Desert

The desert has a beauty all its own
A rustic scene of something to behold
As you look into what the winds have blown
Extend it further out, it does unfold
~ Lady Kathleen

It was 1975 when I first visited my best friend, Lerin, in New Mexico. She introduced me to a tall, fully bearded man with beautiful blue eyes. He wore a big black hat with a long eagle's feather. Although he reminded me of a gentle giant he called himself, "Ivor" after a famous Viking. Ivor was quite a character and one of my greatest teachers.

One beautiful evening at dusk, Ivor drove me to the Sandia Mountains near Albuquerque to witness the sunset. There was no road where he drove his Lincoln Continental as if it was a four wheeler up the mountainside. Ivor played by his own rules. As we silently watched the dusk embrace the land I felt quiet and peaceful. Up until then I never understood why in the world anyone would ever want to live in or even visit a desert. I had grown up near the Pacific Ocean and I always thought of the desert as a hot, barren existence with strange animals and prickly plants.

We watched as bright, breath-taking colors changed like a slide show throughout the sky. We saw cactus and sage brush casting cool colored shadows on the desert below. It was beautiful. After several minutes of serene quiet Ivor gently said, "The desert is like the ocean, Cindy. It is my ocean." My attitude instantly shifted as I found myself in awe of the beauty surrounding us. Ivor was teaching me how to see the desert with spiritual eyes.

As the wind blew softly, we could hear the desert singing her ancient song. It told the story of when she was an ocean and everything we were looking at was once only the mysterious land below her great waters. Now I know why New Mexico is called "the land of enchantment."

Jesus understood the mystical magic of the desert. For forty days and nights he felt the coolness of the evening give relief to the heat of the day. Jesus could hear God's voice whisper to his soul in the song of the gentle desert wind. He completely connected with God as he witnessed the ever changing moon and vast sea of sparkling stars in the darkness of the night. The desert is beautiful at night.

Ivor has passed on but his memory stays with me and I am grateful for knowing him. I wonder if he is enjoying beautiful desert sunsets in heaven. If he is, you can be sure he is saying, "Ahh... How beautiful heaven is! This is just fine."

The Dwarf

"The best way to cheer yourself up
is to try to cheer somebody else up."
~ Mark Twain

Sometimes we briefly meet people that make an everlasting imprint on our lives. To me these people are gifts from God.

I was visiting my daughter, Julie in Grenoble, France. She had opened a little store downtown where she sold Italian Imports.

One afternoon we went to the Post Office to mail some leather journals to some of her customers. At the entrance of the building we saw a dwarf standing with a little tin cup.

He had a forlorn look on his face and my heart went out to him. I was loaded down with packages and my arms were full. I was unable to reach my wallet so I had made up my mind I would fill his empty cup on the way out.

After about 15 minutes we walked outside and the dwarf was gone. It made me sad. I thought to myself, "I should have given him the money when I saw him."

A few days later Julie and I went shopping and she bought a plant for her new home. It had big, dark green leaves and was about 4 feet high. I named the plant Cleopatra.

As I carried Cleopatra down the cobbled stone street I could hear Beethoven's, *Andante Pathetique* playing. It happens to be one of my favorite musical pieces. I remember getting chill bumps the first time I ever heard it. I was thirteen-years-old and had taken my little brothers to see, "A Boy Named Charlie Brown." I knew the music had to be Beethoven because Linus had played the piece in the movie.

A few days later, I sang the first 3 notes to my piano teacher and told him it was written by Beethoven. I learned how to play it within the next two weeks. I even recorded it on one of my piano CDs. I absolutely love that piece of music.

As we walked towards Julie's apartment the music became louder. All of a sudden my heart was filled with excitement. There was the dwarf cranking the handle on a large music box that was playing the musical composition I love so much. In his other hand he was holding the tin cup.

Again my arms were full. I flew up the 5 flights of stairs to Julie's apartment, unloaded the merchandise, grabbed all my change and ran back down to where the dwarf was playing the music box.

It was a weekend and the streets were filled with people shopping. The little dwarf still had that vacant stare on his face and the people walking by were ignoring him. I took all my change and filled his empty cup. Some of the coins fell on the ground. It sounded like a slot machine in Vegas that had just hit the jackpot.

Then to my amazement I heard a sound come out of him that was so loud everyone on the street froze and stared.

A huge eeeeEEEEEEEEEEEE came out of his little body, shrieking with crescendo to a high pitch. His face had transformed into a huge smile! It was the sound of pure joy like no other I have ever even imagined.

I will never forget it! I didn't know a human being could even make a sound like that!

It is a memory that makes me smile.

I hope I get to see that little dwarf in heaven.

If I do, heaven will be just fine!

The Egg Story

"We make all sorts of assumptions
because we don't have the courage to ask questions."
~ Don Miguel Ruiz

I grew up in Southern California at the beach. When I moved to rural East Texas I learned a brand new way of living. Some people might even say it was culture shock.

It was a beautiful fall morning. I was a new bride and I was going cook my cowboy a real country breakfast. I cut up potatoes, onions and green peppers and put them in the oven. In a big black iron skillet I fried bacon and then dropped two eggs in the hot grease. I happen to love them that way.

I made some toast and proudly presented my cowboy with what I thought was a real country breakfast. He looked at it, scrunched up his face and exclaimed, "You scabbed my eggs!"

My bubble was burst. "You don't have to eat it." I said.

TJ, our Doberman, loved it!

From that day, Dennis cooked his own eggs. I just figured he knew how he liked them and it was best for all parties concerned. Finally, after about three years, I attempted again to make his eggs and he was very complimentary!

Over the years we have laughed about the "egg story." Throughout our marriage it has been a great reference to the fact we were both brought up in two completely different worlds.

Fast forward fifteen years!

One Saturday morning, when Dennis was working out of town, he called me laughing.

"I owe you an apology," he said. "I just fried some bacon and dropped a couple of eggs in the hot grease. Those were the best eggs I have ever had!"

"What!" I exclaimed. "You've never tried eggs cooked in bacon grease before??"

I couldn't believe it! One of Dennis's favorite quotes is, "Condemnation without investigation is the epitome of ignorance!"

Now we laugh at the "egg story" even harder.

Life is a beautiful smorgasbord full of choices. Don't miss out on any potential new adventure. You might be missing an opportunity to experience heaven on earth. It will keep you young, interesting and fun to be around.

God created a beautiful world for us to enjoy!

What can you try today that you have never tried before. Maybe you can visit a restaurant, a town or a park you've never been to.

Nowadays, Dennis and I both agree, "If they serve eggs fried in bacon grease for breakfast in heaven, heaven will be just fine!"

The First Light of Dawn

By Cynthia Jordan

It is the darkest hour.
You can hear the silent voice of the night
As the land waits patiently for her arrival
She will come... She always does.
Quietly at first, the sweet songs
Of small-feathered minstrels fill the air
As if announcing, "Her Majesty is approaching!"
From the east a soft glow of light
can be seen on the horizon.
Then, subtly, before all who have the privilege to witness,
The sky is transformed into an exquisite masterpiece!
The lady, being quite the lady,
Very slowly reveals her beauty with grace and style.
Bright magentas and brilliant colors
of fiery orange and gold
exhibit her passions as she paints
a magnificent picture of endless beauty!!
My breath is taken away... She is here!
Her heavenly essence seeks no approval
as she generously lights the new day,
a new beginning for all.
She is not selective and gives unconditionally
as she embraces all of life with her warmth and light.
Her lovely golden rays shimmer through the forest trees
and shine boldly through the clouds.
A gentle peace fills my soul at the First Light of Dawn.

The Play

"...for us physicists believe the separation between past, present, and future is only an illusion, although a convincing one." ~Albert Einstein

Have you ever been in a wonderful dream and then the alarm goes off or something else is going on that makes you realize you are really only dreaming and you don't want to wake up? It's almost like you are in two worlds at once.

Not too long ago I was at my friend, Dale Bowman's 80th birthday party and met Kevin Moen. In the early 80s he played football for Cal State Berkley. In 1982 Kevin made what has been voted "the most memorable touchdown in college football history." It is respectfully referred to as, "The Play".

Cal State had been ahead throughout the game. With 8 seconds on the clock, Stanford had just taken the lead. The Stanford band, assuming the game was over, was in the end zone.

All elements were in perfect flow. With 4 seconds on the clock Kevin made a perfectly synchronized touchdown.

Hundreds of Cal State fans had left the stadium. Those who hadn't left went wild and the roar boomed so loud, the people in the parking lot all turned around and instantly regretted leaving the game! I know because my Uncle Dickie and my brother, Kurt were both there.

I asked Kevin, "Tell me in your words what it was like?"

His eyes filled with light as he began telling me his story as if it had just happened.

"I knew I'd never be in a big stadium again and I wanted to make a touchdown. We didn't really even have a play. I caught the ball and saw my buddy Rodgers over on the side kind of waving to me like this."

With that, Kevin waved his hand in slow motion.

"I threw the ball to Rodgers. When he was getting tackled he threw it to Garner. When Stanford came after Garner he threw the ball back to Rodgers who threw it to Ford. Stanford tackled Ford and on his way down he threw it over his shoulder. I looked up and saw the football. It seemed to be floating in the air, just like that!"

With that, Kevin pointed to a birthday balloon gently floating over the table.

"I caught the football and all I could see was the Stanford Band. I didn't care, I just charged through and I ran with everything I had. I crossed the goal and ran over the trombone player."

"How long did it take," I asked.

"I guess it was about 30 seconds." he said. "But it seemed like forever. Everything was in slow motion."

It was great meeting Kevin. I called my Uncle Dickie who is a HUGE fan and alumni of Cal State Berkley. Guess who I'm with?" I said. "Kevin Moen!"

"O my God!" Dickie exclaimed.

Kevin got on the phone with him and together they went to a mutual moment in time that has made an everlasting imprint in both of their lives. Apparently over 50% of the Golden Bears' fans were headed towards the parking lot when "the play" happened.

"A lot of people claim they saw it," Dickie said with excitement. "I really did!"

When we experience a spectacular, timeless event where all elements are perfectly aligned I like to say, "We are dancing with God."

It's in these magical moments we can truly say, "If this is heaven it would be just fine."

Cindy with Kevin Moen and Uncle Dickie

The Sea

"Love is like the sea.
It's a moving thing, but still and all,
it takes its shape from the shore it meets,
and it's different with every shore."
~ Zora Neale Hurston

One of my favorite stories in the bible is when Jesus calmed the sea. It tells about the time there was a mighty storm and Jesus was sleeping on a cushion in the stern of the boat. The apostles were afraid and woke him up. Jesus understood the ways of the sea, and said, "Quiet, be still!" With that the winds and the water became perfectly calm.

To me the sea is like a beautiful woman. Her cycle is in harmony with the moon and although she can be lovely and serene, she can also be stormy and full of mystery.

The sea is passionate and it is always obvious what mood she is in. Like an elegant woman dressing for dinner, her waters reflect her many moods.

During the day she wears different shades of blue and green. Sometimes she sparkles in the sun and sometimes she is dark and ruffled by a storm. Her evening wear is especially beautiful when the moon and stars shine on her midnight blues and indigo.

Listening to the ocean waves breaking on the shore is like listening to the breath of life itself. When I look from the sea's shore to the horizon I feel an endless connection to God's beauty and majesty.

I grew up in Redondo Beach, California. In any moment I can close my eyes and taste and smell the ocean's healing salty waters, watch a colorful sunset on the horizon, slide down the back of her waves and hear her ancient song. No matter where I am, the ocean is everlasting in my mind.

When I go to Redondo, I love to sit on the sand at sunset. The golden glow on the sand as the light of day makes its transition to the darkness always evokes feelings of peace and appreciation.

Sitting on the shoreline always makes feel close to God and the beauty can move me to tears.

In these magical moments of appreciation, I say with all my heart, "If this was heaven it would be just fine!"

The Wise Young Sage

"After three days they found him in the temple courts,
sitting among the teachers,
listening to them and asking them questions.
Everyone who heard him was amazed
at his understanding and his answers."
~ Luke Chapter 2 vs 46-47

There once was a wise young sage. The elders were jealous of him and his great wisdom. They decided to ask him a question that even the young sage could never answer.

"O young Sage," they said. "We will give you an orange if you can tell us where God is."

The young Sage replied, "I will give you two oranges if you can tell me where God is not."

The story reminds me of how Jesus must have wowed the elders in the temple.

I have received many emails from people saying, "Put God back into schools."

I've got good news for them. God never left!

People who think they can take God out of anything are just silly.

They absolutely cannot win! In fact I have learned their protest deepens our desire to preserve the word, "God".

There are so many synonyms for God. *Love, Peace, Friendship* and *Creator* are all words that explain God.

Even the word "good" as in the phrase, "God is good" says God.

Dog is God spelled backwards. Can you think of a better way to explain unconditional love than a dog??

So, dear friends, don't worry. No one has the power to take God out of anything.

When we say *Love* we are also saying *God*. God is in all of the empty space. If you are in a room, look at all of the empty space! God is there.

Walk outside and there's even more!

It makes me think of the song "I feel it in my fingers I feel it in my toes. Love is all around us and so the feeling grows."

God is all around us.

So next time you hear a frustrated somebody complain about taking God out of schools or anything else, remember the wisdom of the young sage. Comfort them by saying, "Don't worry, it's impossible to take God out of anything." This knowing will bring you peace.

Sometime today may I suggest you try to connect with nature or do something that makes you happy. Then as you feel the peace, love and joy within your heart, smile and say, "If this was heaven it would be just fine."

There's Got to be a Pony!

"A pessimist sees only the dark side
of the clouds, and mopes;
a philosopher sees both sides, and shrugs;
an optimist doesn't see the clouds at all -
he's walking on them."
~Leonard Louis Levinson

"It was the best of times, it was the worst of times,
It was the age of wisdom, it was the age of foolishness,
It was the epoch of belief, it was the epoch of incredulity,
It was the season of Light, it was the season of Darkness,
It was the spring of hope, it was the winter of despair,
We had everything before us, we had nothing before us,
We were all going direct to heaven,
We were all going direct the other way
In short, the period was so far like the present period, that some of its noisiest authorities insisted on its being received, for good or for evil, in the superlative degree of comparison only."

This is the first paragraph in *Tale of Two Cities* written by Charles Dickens in 1859. The story takes place in the time of the French Revolution which occurred from 1789 to 1799. Frankly I think the paragraph is just as true today as well. We live in a world full of contrast. This amazing insight by Charles Dickens reminds me of another story.

There once were six-year-old twin boys who lived in a big fancy house in the country. Peter was a pessimist child and Oscar was an optimist. The boys were put in separate rooms. Peter's room had all kinds of toys and fun things to do. Oscar was put into a room full of horse manure shoveled in from the barn.

Two way mirrors were put on the doors. This way the boys were unable to see out but could be observed from the outside.

Peter was miserable. He kept shaking his head and pouting. When asked why he was so sad he responded, "I don't know which toy to play with first! What if they don't work or break? What if someone comes and takes them all away?"

In the second room they found Oscar laughing and running all around the room as if he was looking for something. Finally he started throwing manure up in the air yelling, "Yippee!"

When asked why he was so happy Oscar responded, "I just know there's got to be a pony in here somewhere!"

I am an optimist. I am always looking for that pony.

I hear so many people who claim that the year 2012 is going to be the end of the world. Sadly many of them are very young.

I say it's just the beginning.

Many people think that we live in a world that is becoming more violent.

Let's take a look at history. People used to go to public executions as entertainment. This is why Nero built the Coliseum. There were actually people on the hills having a picnic at the battle of Gettysburg! During the Spanish Inquisition people took great pleasure in watching people being tortured and killed.

I say the human race is finally learning that *love* really is the best solution.

The fact is, right now, December 2nd, 2011, for the first time in recorded history the statistics show the numbers of war casualties on the planet are greatly reducing.

The internet has the power to unite humanity. Sure there is negative stuff out there but we don't have to be told who to hate anymore. In any moment we can make a friend anywhere in the world.

This is exciting to the optimist.

Which one are you? Do you believe humanity can unite in the spirit of love and harmony and create heaven on earth?

I *know* we can do this together. It only takes 100,000 to unite and begin the mass movement.

I believe children are the answer. It is very enlightening to look at the world through their eyes of wonder. They can teach us so much because they can see heaven on earth. Listen to the wee ones. Their wisdom can blow you away! This is because they are straight from the loving arms of God and have no evil in their hearts.

If you are the optimist you invited to our *Harmony Party*.

If you are the pessimist we invite you to change your attitude or stay home.

We'll still love you.

Just stay home.

Let's do this. Together we can create "on earth as it is in heaven."

Then as we blissfully enjoy our life experience we can surely say, "If this was heaven it would be just fine."

There's No Place like Home

"Life is a journey, not a destination."
~Ralph Waldo Emerson

I love the *Wizard of Oz*. It's a wonderful movie and one of the most spiritually enlightening stories I have ever heard.

Dorothy wants to run away from home because she feels there is something better out there. She gets caught in a tornado and lands in a strange new world.

Dorothy wants to go home. The good fairy comes to her and tells her to follow the yellow brick road. At the end of the road she will find all she is looking for. Somehow, Dorothy finds that she is wearing magical, ruby red slippers.

Dorothy and her little dog, Toto, leave Munchkin Land and she is off on her journey to the Land of Oz to meet the great Wizard.

On the way she meets a Scarecrow who wants a brain, a Tin-man who wants a heart and a Lion who wants courage. The wicked witch wants the ruby slippers and goes after Dorothy. Dorothy finally reaches Oz, meets the Wizard and the witch melts away.

To me the best part of the story is when the good fairy tells Dorothy she has always had the power to go home.

Just click the heels of the ruby slippers and say, "There's no place like home."

After repeating the phrase over and over, Dorothy wakes up, back in her bed in Kansas. Aunt Em, Uncle Henry and all the characters from her journey are there in different form. She tries to tell everyone her journey to Oz wasn't a dream.

In the final line of the movie Dorothy hugs little Toto and repeats, "There's no place like home."

Life is your journey down the yellow brick road. The fairy is your Guardian Angel. We learn to know God through our experiences, our challenges and the people we meet and love.

Are you like Dorothy? Do you think there's something better out there?

There really is no place like home. All of your happiness is here now.

Home is where the heart is. Home is where Love is. Home is where God is and God is with you now. I think if heaven is like what I know as home, heaven will be just fine.

Back Home Again

Words and music by John Denver

There's a storm across the valley,
clouds are rollin' in
The afternoon is heavy on your shoulders
There's a truck out on the four lane a mile or more away
The whinin' of his wheels just makes it colder

He's an hour away from ridin'
on your prayers up in the sky
And ten days on the road are barely gone
There's a fire softly burnin', supper's on the stove
But it's the light in your eyes that makes him warm

Hey it's good to be back home again
Sometimes this old farm feels like a long-lost friend
Yes 'n' hey, it's good to be back home again

There's all the news to tell him, how'd you spend your time
What's the latest thing the neighbors say
And your mother called last Friday,
"Sunshine" made her cry
You felt the baby move just yesterday

Oh the time that I can lay this tired old body down
Feel your fingers feather soft upon me
The kisses that I live for, the love that lights my way

The happiness that livin' with you brings me
It's the sweetest thing I know of,
just spending time with you
It's the little things that make a house a home
Like a fire softly burnin' supper on the stove
The light in your eyes that makes me warm

Now close your eyes and think of a favorite "at home" memory. What do you see? What do you hear? What do you smell?

Where there is love, God is there. Where God is, heaven is and everything is just fine.

Three Fish

"Jesus took the five loaves and two fish,
looked up toward heaven, and blessed them."
Mark 6:41

Every year my dad looks forward to his annual fishing trip with his friends. For weeks, just like every other year, Dad had been on the phone with his friend, Bill and my cousin Danny, planning meals and making a grocery list. I always have enjoyed watching how happy he always is, before his annual fishing trip to Lake Havasu. It's almost as if he is a kid again.

It was May of 2013. Daddy was 84-years-old enjoying his annual fishing trip with the guys. I called Mom. "Have you heard from Dad? Is he having a good time?"

"Your dad is a little discouraged. They haven't caught any fish and they are coming home tomorrow."

I hung up the phone and entered the dentist office where I was about to have my teeth cleaned. As I lay back on the chair, staring at the clever poster on the ceiling that said, *God's Little Blessings,* I started a conversation with God.

"God… how about three fish? I'm just asking for three fish. You know how Daddy loves this fishing trip and looks forward to going every year. Three fish."

That night I called Mom again. "I prayed for dad to catch three fish today. Have you heard from him? Have they caught any fish?"

I could hear Mom smiling over the phone. "You need to call your dad. Here is the number."

I dialed. Bill answered the phone. "Is my dad there? Mom told me to call him."

Dad got on the phone. "Hi, Cindy!"

"Mom told me to call you, Dad. Did you catch any fish today?"

"We sure did! We only caught three but all of them were beauties. Over eight pounds!"

"Really! Three fish. That's great, Dad! Mom wanted me to tell you that I asked God to let you catch three fish today. It sounds like my prayer was answered. I specifically asked for three fish. Don't you just love the way God works?"

"Wonder what would have happened if you had asked for a dozen," Dad said in amazement.

"I guess I could have. Three fish sounded reasonable. Glad you finally caught some fish, Dad. It sounds like they were good ones too."

When a fisherman pulls out a good sized fish I hear it is just like heaven on earth and everything is just fine.

Thumbs Up

"I find hope in the darkest of days, and focus in the brightest. I do not judge the universe." ~ *Dalai Lama*

We were all praying for Danny to get well. These are some of the things I heard people say.

"I'm praying so hard. I pray every day!"

"I know God can fix this!"

"I have faith! I really do."

"Everyone is praying for his healing."

"God can make a miracle!"

"He's a good man. He doesn't deserve to die!"

"I know Jesus can heal him…"

In the cruel days of the Roman Coliseum the emperor would put his thumb down when he wanted a gladiator to kill his opponent. He would put it up if he decided to allow the man to live. Some people might say, "He was playing God."

Wrong!

God doesn't do that.

God doesn't say, "Sure I can heal him but I'm going to let him die. I'm just not feelin' it. Yeah, I hear your prayers but it just wasn't enough to convince me to let him live. Sorry about that. Better luck next time."

God is not human. So why do people give God human qualities?

God is *only* Love.

In times of tragedy love expands. I believe that it is the reason God allows what we judge as, "bad things" to happen. I believe our soul agrees to the human experience because it wants to know love. Sometimes love is most felt in times of great concern. It's when we feel these strong emotions that we turn to God at all.

It makes me think of the destruction of the Twin Towers in 2000. Because of the heartbreak and despair there was a huge expansion of love and unity. Flags were waving and signs everywhere said, "God Bless America!" Where are they now?

Even after the thousands of prayers, my cousin died. My thought was not of sadness. I like to think that the first thing he saw when he went to heaven was his daddy fishing beside the most beautiful crystal clear lake. Danny hadn't seen him since he was ten years old.

"Hey son! I've been waiting for you. Here's a brand new fishing rod. Welcome to heaven, Danny. Hey look... mom and dad are coming. Sure am glad to see you. You know I never really left you. I've been with you for 60 years. You just couldn't see me... Looky there...I gotta bite!"

When we are with those we love we are in heaven. This is because God is love. Heaven is where God is, so heaven is where love is and all is well.

Tita

"Tita, Tita abuelita
Eres mi Tita muy bonita."

Margarita Solis de Hernandez was my grandmother. I was unable to say abuelita when I was small, so I called her, "Tita." Tita taught me unconditional love.

If you had met my Tita in her last days, you would have seen a frail, 90 lb. woman, with cotton white hair, wrinkled skin and no teeth. She had no recognition of her loved ones. However, to those of us who had the privilege of knowing her, we saw an elegant lady who had lived her ninety-seven years with love and passion for life.

Although her mind was gone and her body was failing, Tita's spirit was alive and well. As the nurses came in and out of Tita's room, I wanted to stop each one of them and tell her story. "This is not just any little old lady. This is my Tita! For heaven sakes! She met Pancho Villa when she was three-years-old after he had kidnapped her father and oldest brother and demanded a ransom. She has travelled the world and had an amazing love story with my grandfather, Alberto Solis. You don't realize how awesome this woman is!"

I would shout the words silently from my heart as I watch the kindly hospital staff, patiently tend to her. All of her life, everyone fell in love with Tita. Her eyes always sparkled with love as I watched her blow kisses and tell her caretakers that she loved them. I especially remember Rosa. She called Tita, "Mi Corazon," which means, "my heart."

One day, I remember looking down the hallway of the nursing home and it occurred to me that every room had a Tita. Every frail, hunched over body with cotton white hair had their own unique story filled with love, loss, pain, happiness and life adventures. These people hold the stories of our history and they all have amazing stories to tell.

Many of them lived through the Depression and experienced World War II. They were around before television, studied in one-room school houses and could tell you about a time you could see a picture show and buy a hamburger and a shake, all for about a quarter.

At the end Tita was like a new baby. They fed her pureed food and she would look with wonder around the room as if she saw angels floating around the ceiling. Sometimes she would point and call out to her loved ones who had passed on.

She saw her sisters in white dresses playing with their dolls. She called out to family members and friends. She would smile and laugh as if they were having a party. Tita loved parties!

I'll never forget the day I witnessed this with my uncle.

"Oh Cindy," he said with tender sadness. "Our little Tita is hallucinating."

I smiled back at him, and as the tears filled my eyes, I quietly said, "Just because we can't see them, Uncle Dickie, doesn't mean they're not there."

I'm sure they were all there to welcome her home.

I can just see her in her new, heavenly body as she joined the party. Tita probably said, "Hello Everyone! How beautiful heaven is! This is just fine."

Trees

I think that I shall never see
A poem lovely as a tree.
A tree whose hungry mouth is prest
Against the earth's sweet flowing breast;
A tree that looks at God all day,
And lifts her leafy arms to pray;
A tree that may in summer wear
A nest of robins in her hair;
Upon whose bosom snow has lain;
Who intimately lives with rain.
Poems are made by fools like me,
But only God can make a tree.
~Alfred Joyce Kilmer

God gives us so many beautiful gifts. Look around you. If you are inside you are probably looking at something that was once a tree.

If you are outside you might even be looking at a tree.

One day, while walking in the park, a frustrated friend asked me, "Do you think God ever really hears our prayers?"

I quickly asked God to give me an answer.

"Of course," I said. You are never separate from God. In fact whenever you experience peace, love or joy you are sharing in the essence of God which is a part of your being.

She looked at me kind of funny, like, what in the world are you talking about?

"It's kind of like an oak tree." I said. "From its branches you can create a doll house, a music box, a table, chairs, a violin, a plate, a guitar, a piano and an endless number of other things. Each one has its own purpose different from the other. But then, during a quiet rain, it remembers being the tree. Just as we are made with the essence of God we are one with that essence. Therefore you can never be separate from it."

Suddenly my friend said with excitement, "Cindy, there's a butterfly on your shoulder!" I couldn't see it very well but she could.

As we walked along she kept exclaiming, "It's still there!" The butterfly stayed with us for the rest of the walk. We both saw it as a sign.

"Obviously what I told you was inspired by God," I said. "I'm really not that smart."

I remember looking at the trees all around us and smelling the fresh, clean air. It was a beautiful day of inspiration I will always remember.

Do you think there are trees in heaven?

I'd like to think so.

If heaven has trees, heaven will be just fine.

Thank you God for giving us trees
so we can play music!

Tribes

You have your way. I have my way.
As for the right way, the correct way,
and the only way, it does not exist
~ *Friedrich Nietzsche*

A surprising statistic: Most people would choose death over public speaking. This is pretty crazy. I am a DTM in Toastmasters International. It is the Distinguished Toastmasters Award and the highest honor in the program. I have seen Toastmasters completely transform people into wonderful speakers and communicators.

I have a theory why people hate public speaking. They don't want to be voted off the island! In other words they don't want the tribe to judge them for fear the tribe will reject them. Without the support of the tribe, man cannot survive. At least it's been that way for the first gazillion years.

Things are different now. These days because of our access to the entire globe you can pick the tribe you want to belong to. In America there are several. We are not nomadic anymore. There are grocery stores! You don't have to be dependent on getting your share of the hunt.

With every speech you give in Toastmasters there is an evaluation. This is where another member of Toastmasters gives their personal opinion and finds some kind of suggestion where the speaker can improve. I remember at first I took it personally. Then one day someone said I asked too many question to my audience. The cool thing was, *I didn't agree with her*! I like to ask questions to connect with my audience. This was liberating! In that moment I realized I did not have to be defensive or take suggestions personally. Her opinion was only *her* opinion! I didn't have to agree. Yaay!

There is nothing more liberating than freeing yourself from caring about the "good opinion of others." Somewhere deep in our cellular memory we have the fear of rejection by the tribe for fear of survival. It's OK. We no longer have to be worried about being voted off the island!

Remember you are never alone. God is with you all-ways. All of humanity is just one big tribe. Love really can conquer all. This is how we create heaven on earth. Can you imagine everyone in the world living in harmony! I can see the vision clearly. Then earth would be like heaven and it would be just fine!

Unborn Babies and Music

Music is the mediator between the
spiritual and the sensual life.
~Ludwig van Beethoven

While I was pregnant I talked, read and sang to my babies every day. I even played the piano for them until there was too much baby between my big belly and the keyboard. Babies in the womb have fully a developed sense of hearing at 18 weeks.

The first association we make with the world outside our mother's womb is through our sense of hearing. Hearing is the most dominant of the five senses. Music can help us to emotionally connect and feel more secure in our natural environment. Because of this, unborn babies respond very well when they are exposed to music.

When my daughter, Denise, was fourteen years old, she said something to me one day that convinced me that she recognized the music I played during my pregnancy with her. It was right after I had finished recording the *Peaceful Journey Series.* I could hear that Denise was listening to my CDs on the stereo. She called me into her room and said, "Mommy, every time I hear this one piece, I always play it over and over 8 or 10 times. I don't know why…I just do."

The composition she was referring to is called *A Mother's Heart.* It struck me as pretty amazing that she would recognize the *only* instrumental piece I had written up until the time I was pregnant with her. Until she was seven, I had only written songs with lyrics. Out of over 50 instrumental pieces to choose from, she chose this one particular piece as her favorite. I wrote it in honor of my grandmother, Tita who had bought my first piano for my 11th birthday. It was the first instrumental piece I had written.

Remember that there is only some skin and a little bit of water that separates a baby's ability to hear its outside environment. They can hear *everything* including the negative. Beautiful music creates an ambience of positive emotion that enables the unborn baby to feel content. Playing the same music after they are born will act like a familiar "security blanket" when you lay them down to sleep in their crib. Happy babies make happy families; happy families make happy communities and happy communities make for a peaceful world. A peaceful world would be heavenly.

We're Going to State!

"Ooga Chaka Ooga Chaka Ooga Chaka"

The soccer field looked especially green and the air was filled with the earthy fragrance of fresh cut grass on this beautiful day in Dartmouth, Massachusetts. In just a few hours only one team would win the playoffs and take the title of Southern Massachusetts Soccer Champs. Andy Buckingham was the goalie for the Falmouth All Stars and they were up against the Dighton All Star Team. It was his first year to play soccer.

Dighton was in a different region, and Falmouth had never played them before. When Andy's team saw their opponents running onto the field to warm up, their hearts sank as hope began to drain from their spirits. According to Andy, they weren't just big boys, "They were massive!"

As Andy shares his story, it is as if it happened just yesterday. "It was obvious the Dighton boys had the bigger size advantage. "When we saw them fear began to set in. We knew that if they were as good as they looked, we were in big trouble."

Coach Danielle Faux remained calm while her team started "going nuts." She had coached these boys to this point in the season and knew she had to do something right away. The biggest opponent to the boys was not Dighton, it was the worse opponent of all. The "Fear Monster" was consuming her team! Her boys were intimidated and she needed a solution fast.

Danielle instructed the team to pile into her Ford Explorer. The fourteen-year-old boys were literally piled up on each other. "It was packed!" Then their coach did something brilliant that would help set the tone of the day. She put the Blue Swede recording of Hooked on a Feeling on her music player. The song begins with men chanting Ooga Chaka, Ooga Chaka Ooga Chaka, Ooga Chaka. She cranked it up as loud as she could and the boys began chanting and singing right along.

Danielle played the song several times and with each round the boys became more and more empowered. As the car literally rocked with this newfound energy, the young soccer players took on the mindset of a winning team. It was all-for-one and one-for- all! No longer were they intimidated fourteen-year-old boys. By singing the song in that cramped up little explorer, the Falmouth All Stars had united and transformed into one powerful energy. The fear was gone and they were men on a mission.

The team piled out of the car, fired up to play. There was no more time for thought. They had a game to win. As the boys played soccer, each of them kept the song going in their head and sometimes even sang out loud. "I'm hooked on a feeling! I'm high on believing, that you're in love with me!!" The music put them into a consistent flow of energy and they seemed to be in rhythm with each other.

Andy was the goalie. This was his first season ever to play soccer, and here he was the key defender at an all-star game! There were 63 shots kicked on the goal that day.

As Andy confronted each ball he chanted, "Ooga Chaka, Ooga Chaka." It was the only thing running through his head. Music coupled with intention is an incredibly powerful tool. Andy blocked all 63 kicks.

As for the Dighton All Stars, they had two kicks to their goal. Fortunately for Falmouth, one made it in. That's all they needed. The final score of the game was Falmouth 1, Dighton 0.

After the game Andy learned that his coach, Danielle had never tried using music to empower and unite her team before. No matter where the idea came from, it worked and it worked well. She probably didn't realize how positive the results would be until after the fact. All she knew was that she had a problem and the solution suddenly became clear. She listened to that intuitive voice.

Andy was like a fourteen-year-old kid again. "That day stays with me. Looking back Danielle couldn't have done anything better. We should have been scared. Thought makes us deviate from our natural instincts. By engaging us into the words and the energy of the song, all fear was completely removed. The whole day was overwhelming."

Nothing can ever take a big win away from you. It is your moment, a story you can tell the rest of your life as if it happened yesterday. Andy will always remember that magical day when what he refers to as a "miracle" happened in his life.

Life is a miracle. That soccer field must have been like heave that day…and it was just fine.

What If...

Coincidence is God being anonymous.
~Einstein

It was a sunny day at the beach in September of 2014. My brother Mark and my 27-year-old son, Jordan, were drying off after going for a swim in the ocean at Knob Hill in Redondo Beach. The surf had been unusually rough that week and although that day the waves had settled down to about 4 to 5 feet in the face, they were still strong.

I was sitting on the sand with my daughter Denise who had just learned she was pregnant. The week before, Denise had finished her five year service in the Coast Guard to be with her husband, Dustin, serving as a law enforcer in the Coast Guard in Miami. When she began her career, she had been stationed in Destin, Florida. There, she was on a rescue team that pulled people out of the water when storms would suddenly appear.

"Help!"

"HELP!!"

"Do you hear that?" Denise said. "Someone is in trouble. Listen."

Sure enough we all heard it a very faint, "help" coming from the strong surf about 70 yards away. "It's coming from over there!" Denise pointed.

The sun was glistening bright on the ocean making it almost impossible to see the dark headed teenager bobbing for air. Because it was September, the life guards that were there were watching the beach were at stations several blocks away. No one was at Knob Hill.

Jordan grabbed his fins. All four of us ran towards the desperate cry for help. In less than 30 seconds the fins were on and Jordan made a bee line in the direction Denise was pointing. We could see the lifeguard trucks several blocks away. They could not see the boy. I began frantically waving a towel and dialed 911 on my phone. I dialed three times before it finally connected. Every moment was precious. I saw a work truck by the Knob Hill restrooms race to the lifeguard station three blocks away.

By now there were four others looking out towards the dark headed boy, bobbing in the surf. An older gentleman, wearing a fisherman's hat was on the shoreline gravely concerned.

"Who is that?" he said to Denise, pointing to Jordan who was swimming towards the boy. Jordan had miraculously managed to see the victim through the rough surf bobbing up and down.

"My brother," Denise answered.

"You want to get him killed too!! There is a fierce riptide out there!" the man screamed.

Just then we saw Jordan reach the boy. Years before, my brother Mark had sponsored both Denise and Jordan in the Junior Lifeguard program. Jordan remembered to approach the drowning victim from behind. This is because in their panic there is a good chance they can bring their rescuer down reaching for safety.

Jordan was calm and put his arm around the young boy's neck. "I've got you. Help is on the way. You're going to be okay."

Two minutes later, two lifeguards appeared on the shore. They swam at lightning speed as if they had motors on their fins. One pulled the boy in at an angle, away from the strong current going out to sea. The other lifeguard and Jordan swam in the other direction, parallel to the shore until they were able to avoid the rip tide and come back in.

The older gentleman who had been so concerned was a retired lifeguard. "I just had knee surgery," he winced shaking Jordan's hand. "That boy was drowning. He would be dead if it wasn't for you. Good job son."

All of us were relieved.

One of the lifeguards was talking to the boy, I watched as the poor kid climbed on his bicycle and rode away. He still looked dazed and I think he was a little embarrassed. It was clear he wanted to go home. We never did learn his name.

As we drove home, all of us felt satisfied. "He was dizzy when I got to him, Mom. He had swallowed a lot of water and was about to go under. The rip tide was strong and he was trying to fight it."

"You saved his life, Jordan."

We all began talking about the "What ifs."

What if Mark and Jordan had not come out of the water when they did? They had been swimming closer to the lifeguard station where there were lifeguards and lifeguard trucks several blocks away.

What if Denise had not been trained to hear the boy's cry for help? It was so faint and muffled beneath the pounding of the heavy surf.

What if Jordan had not gone to Junior Lifeguards and known what to do? My brother Mark was actually able to witness the benefit of sponsoring Jordan into the program.

What if...what if... what if?

Reflecting on the event, I can see a beautiful metaphor. When Jordan put his arm around the boy's neck the boy laid his head on Jordan's chest, surrendering to the comfort of his rescuer. "I've got you. You're going to be OK." This is what I hear when I turn my troubles over to God.

"Think about it, Mom," Jordan said later. "That kid's family is not going to be grieving their son at Thanksgiving this year. They will never know how close they came to not having him there."

That would be Jordan.

All of us witnessed God's perfectly orchestrated plan that day. "You're going to be okay." I believe God spoke those words through Jordan. Surrender is a powerful thing. When the young man felt that peace it felt like heaven where everything is just fine.

White Candles

"Love at first sight? I absolutely believe in it!
You've got to keep the faith.
Who doesn't like the idea?
That you could see someone tomorrow
And she could be the love of your life?"
It's very romantic. ~ Leonardo DiCaprio

When I pray I like to light candles. There is something about a small, warm, flickering flame with an intention attached that just makes me feel good. Somehow when I look at the firelight I feel comforted knowing God is acting on my behalf.

Whenever I have a friend who is looking for love in their life I ask them if they feel there is someone they are supposed to be with. Then I tell them to buy a white candle, light it every night and say, "I know you are out there looking for me. This is to light your path to my heart. Thank you God."

You would be surprised at how many of my friends have given me full credit in finding their "soul mate." One of them is my friend Susan. A couple of months after I told her how to find her true love I saw her in the grocery store. She came to me with a great big beautiful smile on her face.

"Cindy!" she said with excitement. "Remember that white candle thing you told me to do?"

"Of course I do," I replied.

"I went home that night and wrote a list of everything I wanted in my soul mate. A few weeks later I was invited to a New Year's Day football party and I met Jerry. I almost didn't go. We started talking in the kitchen and spent the next three hours just talking. We hardly watched any football. Jerry was everything I had on my list including the kind of car he drives!"

I have to admit it kind of freaked me out. That was eight years ago and Jerry and Susan are still together.

Coincidence?

Maybe.

But isn't it more fun thinking the white candle thing worked?

It has worked for just about everyone that's ever tried it. It always surprises me. Sometimes the romance sticks. Sometimes it's a relationship with a powerful lesson.

I once heard that a soul mate isn't someone who also likes Sushi, mountain climbing and walks on the beach. It's a person who comes into your life with an important lesson. I have found that in order to let a new love in, you must let an old love go. Sometimes this means you need to forgive and let go of resentment.

People are attracted to the light of love so make your light shine like a beacon from your heart. When you project unconditional love miracles happen in all different ways. Babies wave at you, butterflies will land on you and then one day you might look up and see that special person you know somehow belongs in your life. I know because it happened to me.

You light the candle. God will take care of the rest.

I wish you love. You know you have found your soul mate when you experience bliss, joy and peace when you are with them. It will feel just like heaven and it will be just fine.

Mom and Dad 1952 Mom and Dad 2015

Writings in the Sand

"People who live in glass houses
should not throw stones."

John 8:3-11 Then the scribes and Pharisees brought to Him a woman caught in adultery. And when they had set her in the midst, they said to Him, "Teacher, this woman was caught in adultery, in the very act. Now Moses, in the law, commanded us that such should be stoned. But what do you say?"

This they said, testing Him, that they might have something of which to accuse Him. But Jesus stooped down and wrote on the ground with His finger, as though He did not hear. So when they continued asking Him, He raised Himself up and said to them, "He who is without sin among you, let him throw a stone at her first." And again He stooped down and wrote on the ground.

Then those who heard it, being convicted by their conscience, went out one by one, beginning with the oldest even to the last.

And Jesus was left alone, with the woman standing in the midst. When Jesus had raised Himself up and saw no one but the woman, He said to her, "Woman, where are those accusers of yours? Has no one condemned you?" She said, "No one, Lord." And Jesus said to her, "Neither do I condemn you; go and sin no more."

"He who is without sin among you, let him throw a stone at her first." Wow! This is one of my favorite Jesus one liners. It was simple yet powerful enough to shift the perspective of an angry mob. Can't you just see them one by one dropping their stones?

So what in the world was Jesus writing in the sand?

Some say Jesus was writing the names and sins of the people in the angry mob, thus fulfilling the prophecy of Jeremiah in the Old Testament.

Jeremiah 17:13 O Lord, the hope of Israel, All who forsake you shall be ashamed. "Those who depart from Me Shall be written in the earth, because they have forsaken the Lord, the fountain of living waters."

That would be a lot to write!

Here is my thought. Maybe Jesus simply wrote, "Thou Shalt Not Kill" in the sand.

Enlightenment is simply remembering we are Divine Loving Beings.

Jesus is the greatest teacher of enlightenment.

Imagine a world where people only love, share and respect each other just as Jesus did.

It is within our power to do these things. Then our world will be just like heaven and it will be just fine.

Who Will Cast the First Stone

Words and music by Cynthia Jordan

Who will cast the first stone, who will walk away
Who will find it in their heart to sit a while and pray
To share the light of a loving God with a troubled soul
Who will cast the very first stone?

We are born in a world full of darkness
We are born in a world full of light
We are all on a journey to remember who we are
It's Love that makes things right

Who will cast the first stone, who will walk away
Who will find it in their heart to sit a while and pray
To share the light of a loving God with a troubled soul
Who will cast the very first stone?

God is there in the loving
God is there when we forgive
We are all on a journey to remember who we are
Now's the time to live!

You Were There

"I feel within me a peace above all earthly dignities,
a still and quiet conscience."
~William Shakespeare

This is a song I wrote dedicated to my daughter, Denise.

You were there all the time
I couldn't see you through the darkness of my mind
I was lost in the cold
You helped me find the light inside my soul
Now my heart can feel
I know that you're the only thing that's real
You loved me through it all you were there
You were there in the night
When all hope for me was gone and out of sight
I was lost I couldn't see
You saved me from drowning in the sea
Now my heart can feel
I know that you're the only thing that's real
You loved me through it all you were there
Now I know you are always here
Your Love surrounds me I have no fear
You were there loving me
When my spirit was longing to be free
I am amazed I saw the light

Now with every breath I know that I'm alive
Now my heart can feel
I know that you're the only thing that's real
You loved me through it all you were there
You love me through it all you are here

God is love and only love. God doesn't make evil happen but God is there when it does, ready to heal and forgive. Just like a small candle in the blackness of a cave, the darker the challenge the easier it is to find the light of God.

God is with us always…all-ways. In the good times and the bad, in sickness and in health, as long as we live forever and ever, Amen

I think my brother-in-law, Danny had the right idea. My husband, Dennis was holding his hands in those last few minutes of his precious life. Hospice was there and peace was all around. Danny was funny up to the last.

"Do you think they have valet service in heaven, brother?"

Dennis smiled. "Yes I do."

Danny nodded his head and soon afterwards, passed through the veil. It was the last thing he said.

Now when I see valet parking I think of Danny. To him it was heaven on earth and it was just fine.

You Are Loved

music and words by Cynthia Jordan

The magic road to happiness is just a thought away
Think about when you were a child remember a happy day
For this was the time we believe dreams can all come true
It's time to remember You Are Loved

(chorus)
You Are Loved from galaxies beyond
You Are Loved sing the sacred song
Open up your mind and listen with your heart
It's time to remember You Are Loved
Let the child take you back to that happy day
When your life was easier and all you did was play
It's a brand new beginning you are born again
It's time to remember You Are Loved

(bridge)
Time is a healer your heart will mend
When you look at the world through the eyes of a child
You can see heaven again
Try to feel the warm embrace from the greatest love of all
Let it fill your troubled soul when you're feeling small
Starlight shines the brightest in the darkest night
It's time to remember
You Are Loved

"We come into this world knowing everything
Remember who you are and all that love can bring."
~ Cynthia

As I forge upon my journey
Moving towards my goal
Sometimes I feel weary
In my body and my soul
It's times like these I turn around
And I always am impressed
With just how far I've come along
Before I stopped to rest

Bright blessings all-ways!
Cynthia

www.ingramcontent.com/pod-product-compliance
Lightning Source LLC
Chambersburg PA
CBHW051817090426
42736CB00011B/1524

* 9 7 8 0 9 8 8 6 5 7 8 6 1 *